GET UP! GET UP!

Open Their Eyes

Devotional with Freedom Exercises for

ATTACKED AT
HME!

a **GREEN BERET'S
SURVIVAL STORY** *of*

the **FORT HOOD
SHOOTING**

JOHN and ANGEL ARROYO
Peggy Corvin, Co-Author

Get Up! Get Up! Open Their Eyes

Design Services by Melinda Martin—Martin Publishing Services

PUBLISHED BY:
Southwestern Legacy Press, LLC
P.O. Box 1231
Gallatin, TN 37066
Stan Corvin, Jr. – Publisher
Email: swlegacypress@gmail.com

ISBN: Paperback – 978-1-7366245-9-3, epub – 978-1-7327625-2-7

LIBRARY OF CONGRESS CONTROL NUMBER (LCCN) 2021920847
LIBRARY CATALOGING:
Get Up! Get Up! Open Their Eyes
Arroyo, Jr., John, M. (John M. Arroyo, Jr.) and Arroyo, Angel (Angel Arroyo) – Authors
Corvin, Peggy (Peggy Corvin) – Co-Author
172 Pages 7 in. × 5 in. (177.8 mm × 127 mm)

DESCRIPTION:
"*Get Up! Get Up! – Open Their Eyes!*" written by John Arroyo, his wife, Angel Arroyo, and Peggy Corvin, a freedom minister holding a Master of Theology degree, supplements *"Attacked at Home: A Green Beret's Survival Story of the Fort Hood Shooting."* It uses the spiritual lessons John and Angel learned as they navigated the labyrinth of hospital stays and medical recovery provided at Fort Sam Houston in San Antonio, Texas. Each lesson includes a personal application freedom guide designed to bring hope to the hopeless and healing to the wounded soul by breaking the chains of long-held strongholds crushing the spirits of so many people. John and Angel's compassion for all people created a desire to tell about the miracles they experienced and to encourage others to see God at work in their lives too. Each lesson in "*Get Up! Get Up! – Open Their Eyes!*" brings new awareness of God's desire to be a strong, ever-present help in the lives of all His children. Since John heard God speak to him in the middle of repeated gunshots and deadly chaos, he uses this supplemental book to encourage us all to hear Him wherever we are. Then we will Get Up and see what He is doing in and through us.

CONTENTS

Part 4 All Things New

Part 5 Open Their Eyes

FOREWORD

I N 2018, WHEN I MET CAPTAIN JOHN M. ARROYO, JR. U.S. Army (Ret.) I was impressed with his big smile and the easy manner with which he carried himself. Knowing that he was a former Green Beret who served in Iraq and Afghanistan, I was not expecting him to be so genuine, sincere, and outgoing. I also knew he was a survivor of the second Fort Hood shooting and expected him to be cynical and a little bitter. But nothing could have been further from the truth as I talked to this kind-hearted and gentle man of God. We soon formed a close bond and personal friendship, especially after he learned that fifty years earlier, I had been a U.S. Army captain serving in South Vietnam as a helicopter pilot, flying combat missions for the 5th Special Forces (SOG).

Once he discovered I had written and published several military memoirs, he asked me to help him with his own manuscript about being shot by a fellow soldier in the second mass murder incident at Fort Hood on April 2, 2014. A year later, I co-authored and published his book, *Attacked at Home: A Green Beret's Survival Story of the Fort Hood Shooting.* The book was an immediate success. John has sold countless numbers of it as he travels worldwide, speaking at military installations and churches about his experience and the faith-enhancing results of his healing and recovery. During his speaking engagements, he has frequently been asked if a devotional or workbook is planned based on the book. Thus, *Get Up! Get Up! Open Their Eyes!* has now been written.

Co-authored by John's wife, Angel Arroyo, and my wife, Peggy Corvin, a freedom minister holding a Master of Theology degree, the new book supplements *Attacked at Home: A Green Beret's Survival Story of the Fort Hood Shooting.* It uses the spiritual lessons John and Angel learned as they navigated the labyrinth of hospital stays and medical recovery provided at Fort Sam Houston in San Antonio, Texas. Each lesson includes a personal application freedom guide designed to bring hope to the hopeless and healing to the wounded soul by breaking the chains of long-held strongholds crushing the spirits of so many people.

John and Angel's compassion for all people created a desire to tell about the miracles they experienced and to encourage others to see God at work in their lives too. Each lesson in *Get Up! Get Up! Open Their Eyes!* brings new awareness of God's desire to be a strong, ever-present help in the lives of all His children. Since John heard God speak to him in the middle of repeated gunshots and deadly chaos, he uses this supplemental book to encourage us all to hear Him wherever we are. Then we will Get Up and see what He is doing in and through us.

With Kind Regards,

Stan Corvin, Jr.
Publisher – Author

INTRODUCTION

In *Attacked at Home: A Green Beret's Survival Story of the Fort Hood Shooting* Angel and I told our journey about God's Power and Mercy in our lives as He healed, restored, redeemed, and set us free. In an abundance of Grace, He has continued to amaze us, as He has used our story to go beyond our immediate family into the world.

As we prayed over the development and publication of the book; we also prayed for you. Moving into the next part of the God-led journey of our lives, we have heard testimonies of how God is revealing His endless love to others through what He did in us.

We are very aware everyone has a different journey. You probably didn't get attacked by an active shooter, but you probably are aware of being spiritually attacked. There are many stories of lives submerged in darkness because of these attacks. Since you are reading this book, you are probably searching for the way to find hope amid hopelessness.

We have been prompted to develop this guide to accompany our first book. Angel and I were led to work with Peggy Corvin, Freedom Minister, and author[1], to set down some spiritual insights into the ways of achieving personal Freedom. We became aware that even after Jesus had reached down and touched our hearts, we were stuck in strongholds that were keeping us from walking in the Freedom He had come to give us. With each devotional entry, there will be freedom exercises to lead you to

- See your life from a God-perspective
- Feed your inner spiritual person with the Word
- Strengthening your will to follow Jesus' ways

These exercises are to be used during your time with God and will guide you to

- Read the Word of God prayerfully
- Reflect on what Holy Spirit is saying to you through that word
- Record your insights and understandings as you hear from the Lord

Every anecdote, every problem, every past hurt, every changed direction told in these pages reveals that God was

---

1 *Diamond in the Darkness: Abused Child of Darkness, Reclaimed Daughter of Light by Peggy Corvin, MPT*

drawing us to Jesus even when we didn't know it. Every victory, every solution, every celebration, every good and perfect thing in our lives reveals the faithful goodness of God. Since Eden, the desire of His heart has been to be our God and for us to be His children so He can come and live among us. Jesus made the way for that to happen. When we live our lives on Purpose—His purpose—we will fulfill the desire of Our Father's Heart.

May you be blessed by each writing. Our prayer for the work contained in these pages is for each person, as they close the book in completion, to say from a knowing heart, "I am the Beloved's, and He is mine."

—John M, Arroyo and Angel Arroyo, Authors
—Peggy Corvin, Co-Author

†††

PART 1

GET UP!

"Get up. Stand on your feet.
I have chosen you to work for Me."

—Acts 26:16

TURNING POINT

WHERE WERE YOU WHEN EVERYTHING CHANGED? I thought I knew where I was going that day. I was on my way to the battalion supply office. I thought I knew what I needed; organizational property information so I could complete an important training exercise.

Where was God? Looking back, I can see His hand in every moment. The parking lot was full, and seconds ticked off the clock as I searched for an open spot. Those seconds counted. The spot that opened up was near my brigade headquarters. I stepped out of my car just as shots rang out and time slowed down. I turned my head and unknowingly looked at the car of the perpetrator of evil, but then turned away to look at the road. It was in that moment the .45 caliber bullet ripped through my throat, severed my left jugular vein, traveled through my voice box, and embedded in my right shoulder and arm.

God prompted the turning away. Had I stood there and stared at that man, he could easily have fired a bullet that ripped through my head. My story would have ended

7

in that parking lot. God didn't cause me to get shot that day. Because He is all-knowing, however, He knew the attack was coming. He will never waste a single act of evil in our lives. He will use it to reveal more of His character and nature than we have ever known before.

He knew I wasn't following closely after Him and He would use this great evil to an advantage to bring me closer to Himself. He tells us He is a jealous God. He longs for us to draw near to Him so He can be near to us. Looking back through my life, I can see time after time He tried to bring me closer. Person after person was sent to model His ways and invite me to do the same. He nudged me to look for Him, even using my grandma's anointing oil to show me His Power while I was deployed. But I kept pushing Him away. The world had a stronghold on me. The devil's wiles were still enticing me. The devil's lies had become my truth. God knew I needed a different source of supply for my life, and a different kind of information because He had a different training in store for my life.

It was time for a turning point for me. He had recently opened up a new life in Texas and had sent some more great, godly, inspiring people in my life. But He knew it was time for me to stop living a Christian life vicariously through others. It was time to come and KNOW God heart to heart.

It was time to turn to Him and let go of everything else. It was time to surrender it all so He could give me everything that would ever matter.

God intervened and saved my physical life that day. He did it because He wanted to save my soul so He could give me abundant life. God loved me that much! Just like He loves you that much too.

**Freedom Exercise:
Read, Reflect, Record**

These exercises are designed to lead you into deeper communication with God. The Word of God is alive and helps us understand what is of our soul, and what is of God's Spirit. As you begin, pray, and tell God you need His help to gain understanding and insights from His Word. Ask for more of Holy Spirit within you to reveal any hidden things. There is no time frame for each of these. Sometimes these entries will lead you into very deep soul work with the Lord and they may require your attention for several days. Sometimes an entry may be completed in only one session with The Lord. Write out your reflections in a journal or a notebook so you can refer back to them.

As you read through each of these Scriptures personalize them. Read them as a conversation you are having with God.

> You formed my innermost parts; You knit me together in my mother's womb. I will give thanks and praise to You, for I am fearfully and wonderfully made; Wonderful are Your works, and my soul knows it very well. My frame was not hidden from You, when I was being formed in secret,

and intricately and skillfully formed in the depths of the earth. Your eyes have seen my unformed substance; and in Your book were all written the days that were appointed for me, when as yet there was not one of them even taking shape. How precious also are Your thoughts to me, O God! How vast is the sum of them! If I could count them, they would outnumber the sand.

—Psalm 139:13–18

While we were still helpless and powerless to provide for our salvation, at the right time Christ died as a substitute for the ungodly. Now it is an extraordinary thing for one to willingly give his life even for an upright man, though perhaps for a good man, one who is noble and selfless and worthy, someone might even dare to die. But God clearly shows and proves His own love for us, by the fact that while we were still sinners, Christ died for us. Therefore, since we have now been justified, declared free of the guilt of sin, by His blood, how much more certain is it that we will be saved from the wrath of God through Him. For if while we were enemies we were reconciled to God through the death of His Son,

> it is much more certain, having been reconciled, that we will be saved from the consequences of sin by His life. That is, we will be saved because Christ lives today.
>
> —Romans 5:6–10

> We love Him because He first loved us.
>
> —I John 4:19

1. Reflect on your turning point. Angel and I have shared that we could see how God used a situation to bring us to Him. What happened on your journey to bring you to a point where you encountered the Living God? Ask God to show you all the ways He guided you to that point.

2. Ask God **why** He guided you to Him.

3. Refresh the joy you feel because you were saved by Him.

DECISION POINT

THE DAY I WAS SHOT, JESUS COULD HAVE OPENED up heaven, touched me, and in a holy moment healed my body. He could have reached down from heaven and picked me up. He didn't.

He said, "Get up! Get up, or your wife will die." He was giving me a choice. He wanted to know if I would believe Him so that I could stay alive and keep my wife and children from death and destruction. Or would I believe the overwhelming condition of my body and give up and die.

That split-second moment when I heard the voice of God will last forever in my mind and heart. That moment has brought me so much clarity and insight because that opened up my spiritual eyes.

First of all, He gave me a command, "*Get Up!*" Had anyone else told me to get up I would have told them, "*I can't!*" In fact, I will tell you today; I couldn't get up at that moment. I was bleeding out, extremely weak, and I couldn't call out for help. A .45 caliber bullet delivers a tremendous amount of pain. My chest felt as if some big guy had hit me with a baseball bat. I had never felt paralyzing pain before, but I know I will never forget how it felt. I was in a hopeless situation without any possible way to save myself.

"*Get up! Get up, or your wife will die!*" Jesus knows everything from the past, present, and future. I knew the emotional condition my wife was in, and Jesus knew I knew. He was moved to compassion for her and believed my compassion for her would prompt me to choose to live. I would choose to do something for her that I couldn't do for myself.

"*Jez... Jez...*" was the only sound I could get out of my mouth as I tried to pray to Jesus. I had a sudden memory of my pastor teaching us to pray out loud. I couldn't even do that. But because He heard the prayer in my heart, He helped me.

Using my left hand to stem the flow of my blood that was pouring to the ground, since my right arm was completely useless, I miraculously got to my feet and sought help. Since I responded to Jesus' spoken command, He met me in my weakness and gave me the strength to go find help. Because I got up, soldiers could see me and rushed to help. Had I stayed on the ground I would have bled out.

I had to come to a place where I knew I couldn't save myself. I had to have Jesus. I live because Jesus invited me to choose to Get Up. He let me decide; getting up was the best decision I have ever made.

Freedom Exercise: Read, Reflect, Record

Pray and ask Holy Spirit to highlight the key points as you read and meditate on each of these Scriptures.

Remember what it says:

> Today when you hear his voice, don't harden your hearts as Israel did when they rebelled.
>
> —Hebrews 3:15

> Jesus responded, "Didn't I tell you that you would see God's glory if you believe?"
>
> —John 11:40

1. Spend time in prayer about whatever you are holding on to that is keeping you from seeing God's glory in your life. As you do, ask God to speak into it; what is He saying to you? Holy Spirit wants to reveal any hardened places in your heart if you will ask.

> "Today I have given you the choice between life and death, between blessings and curses. Now I call on heaven and earth to witness the choice you make. Oh, that you would choose life, so that you and your descendants might live!
>
> You can make this choice by loving the Lord your God, obeying him, and committing yourself firmly to him. This is the key to your life. And if you love and obey the Lord, you will live long in the land the Lord swore to give your ancestors Abraham, Isaac, and Jacob."
>
> —Deuteronomy 30:19–20

2. I knew I had to have Jesus save my life because I couldn't do it. What is in your life that no matter what you do isn't getting any better? Ask God to show you what you have been trying to do that He wants to do for you. What do you need to turn over to Him so He can breathe life into it?

3. Once we acknowledge we can't do it, we must make a conscious decision to turn it over to Jesus. God always lets us choose: life or death, blessings or curses. Pray and tell Him what your decision is today.

4. Ask Holy Spirit to help you strengthen your will to follow through on your decision.

IMPOSSIBLE TO HIM-POSSIBLE

WHEN I GAVE MY LIFE TO JESUS, I WAS AN improbable disciple. Nothing in my past would have indicated that I was disciple material. In fact, it was impossible for me to be anything like Jesus.

My list of credentials inspired concern instead of confidence. I was a fatherless kid who fathered a kid at 15. A gang member, a drug addict, a failure on my first attempt to test into the military; a marginal soldier by finally scoring a mere one point more than I needed to qualify. The military began to shape me, and I gained some skills and had some successes. But even then, I was failing at the things that really mattered. I was often angry with my wife and my kids. Rather than lovingly teaching them and leading them, I dictated, yelled at them, and pushed them away, causing division in our family. I still liked to drink and party with friends, even when I was stumbling into church the morning after to marginally participate in the Christian culture. During all that chaotic time, I had one false "friend" who wanted to be my companion, and his name was satan.

After I decided to say yes to Jesus and put my failures behind me, there was still a struggle. I had to fight to heal my body. Jesus miraculously kept me from dying, He called my name and called me to him. However, my body had received what should have been a "mortal wound." The effects of that wound required time, and medicine, and restoration so I could fully live.

In the same way, Jesus was reaching into my soul healing the mortal wound my enemy satan had tried to deliver to it. It would take time to heal my soul wounds, too. Our Father could have spoken "Universe!" and the worlds would have formed by the Power of His Voice. But He didn't. He took six days to form everything in the perfect right way. He is a God of process so we can see more of His nature and character through His process.

The spiritual medicine my soul was fed was the Living Word of God. The more I read, the more I wanted to read because it was revealing Jesus to me in a way I had never known before.

The restoration began as Jesus showed me His truth about my past. There were some painful situations I had to revisit; He went with me and guided me in my understanding. More restoration came as I admitted what I had done to other people; it was so healing to ask for and receive their forgiveness. He also helped me let go of the hurts I had clung to for far too long as He led me to forgive others. His grace and mercy during this process of being forgiven and forgiving others opened my heart so I could also forgive myself.

True forgiveness would have been impossible without Him. But I have so much joy and compassion for other people because He led me to, and guided me through, this restoration process.

God met me when I was an *impossible* guy serving as a Green Beret pledged to "De Oppresso Liber" (Freeing the Oppressed). He has freed me and is growing me to be a Him-possible soldier in the Kingdom of Heaven's Army.

**Freedom Exercise:
Read, Reflect, Record**

Spend time in these Scriptures, letting them speak to your soul.

> The thief comes only to steal and kill and destroy; I have come that they may have life and have it to the full.
>
> —John 10:10 NIV

1. How has satan attacked you in your life? Ask Holy Spirit to show you what your enemy has tried to steal from you. What has he tried to kill, maybe not physically, but perhaps relationships, opportunities, stability? What do you feel has been destroyed because of satan's influence in your life?

> Once you were dead because of your disobedience and your many sins. You used to live in sin, just like the rest of the world, obeying the devil—the commander of the powers in the unseen world.

He is the spirit at work in the hearts of those who refuse to obey God. All of us used to live that way, following the passionate desires and inclinations of our sinful nature. By our very nature we were subject to God's anger, just like everyone else.

But God is so rich in mercy, and he loved us so much, that even though we were dead because of our sins, he gave us life when he raised Christ from the dead. (It is only by God's grace that you have been saved!)

For he raised us from the dead along with Christ and seated us with him in the heavenly realms because we are united with Christ Jesus.

—Ephesians 2: 1–6

2.   When your heart is ready to, ask Jesus to take you into each of those situations to show you how He sees them. Ask Him for wisdom to know how He wants to restore the things the enemy has taken from you. How does He want to heal your soul wounds?

> "The Spirit of the Lord is upon Me, Because He has anointed Me To preach the gospel to the poor; He has sent Me to heal the brokenhearted, To proclaim liberty to the captives And recovery of sight to the blind, To set at liberty those who are oppressed.

—Luke 4:18

3. As we become restored followers of Jesus, then God will show us what He has anointed us to do. Ask Him how you are to complete the sentence:

    The Spirit of the Lord is on me because He has anointed me to _____.

WHAT ARE YOU
WAITING FOR?

FOR MONTHS AFTER I WAS SHOT, I STRUGGLED
with how to create a new life. I knew Jesus had called me to
come and live a transformed life, but I didn't wake up every
morning with Scripture, or affirmations, or a new view of
who I was.

At first, the course of my days was determined by my
physical recovery. I started with an accountability forma-
tion in the morning followed by various appointments
designed to help me reach my medical goals and keep me
moving toward my career objectives. I was also assigned
to a counselor to help me deal with the residual fear that
had settled over me because I had been shot by someone
wearing the same uniform while I was on one of the most
secure military installations in the world. All these efforts
were instrumental in my physical and emotional recovery.
My body has finally healed, leaving behind many scars.
My emotions have been greatly healed even though some
situations still trigger a sense of fear.

After this traumatic event happened in my life, at some point I had to ask a two-part question. "Who am I now?" and "Who do I want to be?"

There were many options. I could have clung to the identity of "victim" which carries with it many labels; *failure, damaged, limited, "why me" mentality, and incapable.* I could have chosen from a myriad of emotions to define me; *angry, bitter, depressed, etc.* I could have just chosen to stuff it all down and let alcohol and drugs come back into my life to numb it all.

Jesus kept working on my heart and helped me find a new direction. When you have heard the audible voice of the Creator of the Universe, it causes a strong desire in your soul to tell other people about how He saved you. Since I wore a sling for approximately two and a half years, Jesus used it as a conversation starter. When someone asked me about it, I was given the opportunity to share how Jesus saved my life. The more I shared about Him, the more I wanted to get closer to Him. The more I read the Bible, the more He highlighted in His Word. One day, a revelation came through two Scriptures that at first didn't seem to be connected.

From the New Testament, I saw the account of Jesus encountering a man lying beside the pool that was to bring him his healing:

> "Soon another Feast came around and Jesus was back in Jerusalem. Near the Sheep Gate in Jerusalem there was a pool, in Hebrew called Bethesda, with five alcoves. Hundreds of sick people—blind, crippled, paralyzed—were in these alcoves. One man had been an invalid there for thirty-eight years.
>
> When Jesus saw him stretched out by the pool and knew how long he had been there, he said, "Do you want to get well?"
>
> The sick man said, "Sir, when the water is stirred, I don't have anybody to put me in the pool. By the time I get there, somebody else is already in."
>
> Jesus said, "Get up, take your bedroll, start walking." The man was healed on the spot. He picked up his bedroll and walked off."
>
> —John 5:1–8 MSG

In the Old Testament it is recorded that Israel wandered in the wilderness, wanting to get to go live the life God had promised them:

"Thirty-eight years passed from the time we first left Kadesh-barnea until we finally crossed the Zered Brook! By then, all the men old enough to fight in battle had died in the wilderness, as the Lord had vowed would happen. The Lord struck them down until they had all been eliminated from the community."

—Deuteronomy 2:14–15

Jesus asked me, "John, do you want to be healed so I can transform your life?" I knew He didn't mean physically; He meant Spiritually.

"Yes, Lord," was my resounding answer.

"Then what is it you are waiting for, and holding on to, and identifying yourself with that has to die so I can fulfill My promises in your life?"

I had to stop being paralyzed by my current situation. I had to stop waiting on other people, other ways, other ideas to transform my life. I had to get up and get in the Living Water; immerse myself in Him, His words, His ways.

I had to let the old ways of doing things die out there in the wilderness that had been my life. I had to get up out of the battle against flesh and blood and join Jesus in the fight to defeat satan and the old ways so His Promises could be born in me!

Freedom Exercise:
Read, Reflect, Record

Spend time reflecting on the John 5:1–9 and Deut. 2:14–15

1. What area of your life needs healing? Prayerfully answer Jesus' question, "Do you want to be healed?"

2. Ask Holy Spirit to show you what excuse you are using to keep you from receiving His healing. Who or what have you looked to make your life better? Who or what have you blamed for keeping you in this situation?

3. Ask Him how you can participate with Him in bringing about His will in this. Ask Him to show you what you are waiting on, and why.

4. Ask Holy Spirit to show you what there is in you that **must** die in order for God's plan to unfold in your life.

5. Write out a commitment to yourself to get up out of the old and claim your new life.

FREEDOM IN
THE MIDDLE OF THE PRISON

As I began to follow Christ, I was still living in some of the same old situations with family and friends. When I was shot, some of them probably thought I was just getting what I deserved because of all the bad things I had done. They were probably just waiting for me to return to my old ways.

This part of the transformation of my life was sometimes hard to navigate. I still looked like the old drugged-out gang member complete with tattoos. I had listened to satan for so many years he had tattooed his lies on my mind. The last thing satan wants is for Jesus to transform our minds. However, Scripture tells us that, *Where the Spirit of the Lord is, there is Freedom*; and that, *If the Son sets you free, You are free indeed!*

Insight for me came through the story of Paul and Silas found in Acts Chapter16. They had upset the world around them because they cast a demon out of a woman who was earning lots of money for her masters.

The world system is often corrupt and when God's Light shines into those places it reveals the darkness. Anytime that happens, the people that are comfortable in the darkness will always push back.

The masters lied about Paul and Silas and had them stripped, beaten, thrown into the innermost dungeon, and bound by ankle chains. Instead of giving up and going along with what the world thought they deserved, they began to pray and sing hymns to God. Anytime we get up out of dark situations, pray from believing hearts, and praise Him *no matter what*, everything can change in a holy instant.

God caused an earthquake that shook the prison, broke the shackles, and threw wide-open the doors. Those two godly men could have run out of the prison and never looked back. Instead, they used their freedom to serve and to save. When the jailer asked, *"What must I do to be saved?"* They replied, *"Believe in the Lord Jesus and you will be saved, along with everyone in your household."*

Like me, you may still be bound by family ties, work situations, and many other things to people who only know you the way you once were. You may still be in a type of prison built by your past choices. You may be imprisoned by anxiety or depression. But when we get up, raise our voice in worship like Paul and Silas, and believe that Jesus is with us, then no matter what the "prison" looks like, He can shake off everything that is keeping us bound.

Our lives may seem scary and uncomfortable at first, but we have been given His word that when we believe in Him, we *and all our household* will be saved.

**Freedom Exercise:
Read, Reflect, Record**

One day as we were going down to the place of prayer, we met a slave girl who had a spirit that enabled her to tell the future. She earned a lot of money for her masters by telling fortunes. She followed Paul and the rest of us, shouting, "These men are servants of the Most High God, and they have come to tell you how to be saved."

This went on day after day until Paul got so exasperated that he turned and said to the demon within her, "I command you in the name of Jesus Christ to come out of her." And instantly it left her.

Her masters' hopes of wealth were now shattered, so they grabbed Paul and Silas and dragged them before the authorities at the marketplace. "The whole city is in an uproar because of these Jews!" they shouted to the city officials. "They are teaching customs that are illegal for us Romans to practice."

A mob quickly formed against Paul and Silas, and the city officials ordered them stripped and beaten with wooden rods. They were severely beaten, and then they were thrown into prison. The jailer was ordered to make sure they didn't escape. So the jailer put them into the inner dungeon and clamped their feet in the stocks.

Around midnight Paul and Silas were praying and singing hymns to God, and the other prisoners were listening. Suddenly, there was a massive earthquake, and the prison was shaken to its foundations. All the doors immediately flew open, and the chains of every prisoner fell off! The jailer woke up to see the prison doors wide open. He assumed the prisoners had escaped, so he drew his sword to kill himself. But Paul shouted to him, "Stop! Don't kill yourself! We are all here!"

The jailer called for lights and ran to the dungeon and fell down trembling before Paul and Silas. Then he brought them out and asked, "Sirs, what must I do to be saved?"

They replied, "Believe in the Lord Jesus and you will be saved, along with everyone in your household."

—Acts 16:16–31

1. Where in your life do you feel imprisoned, and bound?

2. This account of Paul and Silas reminds us that even in the darkest, hardest places, God is there with you and is only a prayer away. When we take our eyes off where we are today and look to God to show us where He wants to take us, miraculous restoration and reconciliation can happen. Spend time with Him praising Him and asking for His help.

> Through Him, therefore, let us at all times offer up to God a sacrifice of praise, which is the fruit of lips that thankfully acknowledge and confess and glorify His name.
>
> —Hebrews 13:15

3. Praising God in the middle of a hard battle shows you are choosing to have more faith in Him and His power and promises and goodness than you have in a problem or a current situation. Ask God to show you where you have more faith in the strength of your problem than you do in Him.

He said with tears in his eyes, "Lord, I have faith. Help my weak faith to be stronger!"

—Mark 9:24

4. This verse is a quote from a father who came to Jesus saying, *"If you can"* please heal my son. This is often an honest statement from our heart when we are going through difficult things that look as though there is no good solution available. We admit we believe, but we need help believing fully that He will help us. When we can't even see an answer, we need to look to the only One who can. Jesus responded with compassion for that father. He wants to do the same for us all; He is willing to strengthen our faith, particularly when we ask. Ask Him today.

WHERE WILL YOU
PUT YOUR FAITH?

THE MOMENT OF THE GREATEST MIRACLE IN MY life came during shots fired which caused chaos and fear to take hold and spread all around me. For a long time after the shooting, I was left with a fear of being randomly and unexpectedly attacked again. Early in my recovery as I walked by people, I sometimes wondered if the person that just passed would attempt to shoot me in the back. If a vehicle drove slowly by me, I would wince when I saw it.

The broadcast news on any given day will contain reports of active aggressors spread across the world. Additionally, there is a confusing attack from a deadly virus causing concern and worry. All these reports can bring with them a gripping fear and anxiety. If we focus on them, we can feel hopeless and depressed.

Reading the Bible, I found verse after verse saying do not fear, or fear not. Why did God need to keep telling people not to fear? There are 365 verses addressing fear: one for every day of our year. Why do we need that many reminders?

I believe it is because the enemy of our soul, the one who would rob us of all our peace and joy, uses fear to try to block our faith in God.

When I lay on the ground dying, God spoke to me and saved my life. I personally experienced the mighty power of God in my life. Yet, I had to process through that residual fear. In a Psalm everyone knows, David said, *"Yea, though I walk through the valley of the shadow of death, I will fear no evil;"* When I came through that same valley, fear tried to come with me out of that experience. He goes on to say why he doesn't fear. *"For You are with me; Your rod and Your staff, they comfort me."* David had been a shepherd and he knew that a rod and a staff were tools to be used to gently tap the sheep to get them to go onto the path that was best for them. The sheep needed to be guided during the most dangerous areas on the paths. It was only from the shepherd's vantage point that they could be kept safe and find their way. David knew God was with him because He had given him the power to kill a lion, a bear, and a giant enemy warrior, and he knew God would never leave him.

God spoke through Moses to show us the source of our reassurance in these dark times.

> *"When you go out to fight your enemies and you face horses and chariots and an army greater than your own, do not be afraid. The LORD your God, who brought you out of the land of Egypt, is with you!"*

—Deuteronomy 20:1

Jesus also told us He would never leave us. He takes up residence in our hearts and Holy Spirit comes to comfort and to give us wisdom. As He was telling his disciples He was leaving earth Jesus said,

> *"The Helper, the Holy Spirit, whom the Father will send in My name, He will teach you all things, and bring to your remembrance all things that I said to you. Peace I leave with you, My peace I give to you; not as the world gives do I give to you. Let not your heart be troubled, neither let it be afraid."*

—John 14:26–27

The Son of God lives with us with power greater than we can imagine, with love for each of us that defies all reason, and with wisdom to give us to overcome any and every obstacle in our lives. Since He is for us, there is nothing that can defeat us.

Paul, writing to Timothy identified the source of what could keep us from walking in that victory.

> I remember your genuine faith, for you share the faith that first filled your grandmother Lois and your mother, Eunice. And I know that same faith continues strong in you. This is why I remind you to fan into flames the spiritual gift God gave you when I laid my hands on you. For God has not given us a spirit of fear and timidity, but of power, love, and a sound mind.

The spirit of fear is one of the fourteen named demons in Scripture. It is of the devil, and it does not come from God. When we look at all the alarming situations in the world and believe in the power it seems to have to destroy us, we invite the devil to release his spirit of fear into our lives. Genuine faith, true belief in the power and love of God to defend and protect us, tramples that demon and fixes our mind on Jesus.

Since we are serving together in the Spiritual Special Forces there is an important insight to be found in Moses' instructions in Deuteronomy 20 about warfare, *"Then the officers will also say, 'Is anyone here afraid or worried? If you are, you may go home before you frighten anyone else.'* Jesus echoes this concept, saying *"He who is not with Me is against Me, and he who does not gather with Me scatters abroad."* We are called to be in unity with each other against our common enemy and for Our Lord. We are called to hold our thoughts in obedience to all Jesus has told us, to have genuine faith **in Him**, and to speak words that encourage and lift up those with us on this journey.

We must all decide where we will place our faith. Will we believe in the power of darkness, or will we believe in Our All-powerful Savior?

Freedom Exercise:
Read, Reflect, Record

> There is no fear in love; but perfect love casts out fear, because fear involves torment. But he who fears has not been made perfect in love.
>
> —1 John 4:18

1. Today, consider the perfect love of Jesus. Ask Holy Spirit to show you any area where you are questioning His love for you personally.

2. Prayerfully bring any area of anxiety before the Lord and ask to hear what He has to say about the fear you are feeling.

> Then Jesus got into the boat and started across the lake with his disciples. Suddenly, a fierce storm struck the lake, with waves breaking into the boat. But Jesus was sleeping. The disciples went and woke him up, shouting, "Lord, save us! We're going to drown!" Jesus responded, "Why are you afraid? You have so little faith!" Then he

> got up and rebuked the wind and waves, and suddenly there was a great calm.

3. Are there any "storms" in your life right now? Where do you feel that you will be destroyed by the constant "waves"? Open your heart in prayer and be completely honest with the Lord.

4. Consider this: the disciples were afraid they were going to perish by the fierce storm while Jesus slept in their same boat. What boat will *ever* sink when Jesus is onboard? Have you invited Jesus onto your boat? Ask Him to show you how to work with Him to rebuke the source of the storm.

5. Admit that you need more faith in Him and less in the circumstances of your life. Let your heart cry be for an increase of faith in Him. Faith is not just believing He *can* do something; it is believing He *will* do it for you! Are you putting your faith in His ability, or in His great motivating love for you?

†††

PART 2

LOOK UP!

They looked to Him and were radiant,
And their faces were not ashamed.

—Psalm 34:9

SOUL PROSPERITY

IN YEARS PAST, MANY CHURCHES EXPERIENCED explosive growth as they taught what came to be known as a prosperity gospel. Basically, it was taught that all you had to do was tithe abundantly and God would provide everything you wanted. It was an errant teaching. A tithe is a heart action acknowledging that God has provided all we have, by returning a tenth to Him for use in the kingdom. God's character never shows that we must "give to get."

He does want to provide for us, but His focus is always on our greater good. He wants us to have all the good things of life. Jesus said, *"I have come that they may have life, and that they may have it more abundantly."* The Greek word for life in that verse refers to physical life in the present time as well as our eternal spiritual existence.

God desires that all His children should have "Shalom." Often translated as "Peace," it is that, yet so much more. It speaks of completeness, fullness, and wholeness in every area of our lives. Jesus came so we could thrive in our life;

relationships, marriages, finances, health, careers, and all things.

The more I followed Jesus, the more I realized the world had never shown me how to live a satisfying life. He is not the fun squasher. He is the Way, the Truth, and the Life. His words to me when He said, "Get Up," will always be with me, and they highlight things differently in Scripture. I noticed that when Jesus taught his closest followers it was only after they went "up" the mountain. When God called Moses to come to Him so He could give him the instructions for people to be able to live abundant lives, He called him to come "up" to Him.

Everywhere I go, I meet people who are just like me. People are looking for hope, peace, freedom, and abundantly full lives. I tried everything I knew to try, and nothing worked; my life was a mess. Only when I gave myself over to Jesus did I realized the lies I had believed about Him. I have shed the lies and I have truly begun to live.

There is grace and mercy for us all. Jesus didn't come to condemn the world, but to save it. He loved us enough to take all our sins to the cross. He also loves us too much not to show us the more excellent way to live. He came to tell us to repent and return to the commandments so we can live as God's children. He said:

"Do not think that I have come to abolish the Law or the Prophets; I have not come to abolish them but to fulfill them. For truly I tell you, until heaven and earth disappear, not the smallest letter, not the least stroke of a pen, will by any means disappear from the Law until everything is accomplished."

Jesus fulfilled the law by being our sacrifice and then sent Holy Spirit to live inside every born-again Christian to motivate our transformed hearts to live in obedience to Christ and glorify God the Father.

God's ways are higher than our ways and we can only understand his ways when we commit ourselves to come up higher and seek Him.

Finally, God's plan is for you to prosper. Follow what He told Joshua and you too will prosper and have good success.

"This Book of the Law shall not depart from your mouth, but you shall meditate in it day and night, that you may observe to do according to all that is written in it. For then you will make your way prosperous, and then you will have good success."

Freedom Exercise:
Read, Reflect, Record

> And seeing the multitudes, He went up on a mountain, and when He was seated His disciples came to Him.
>
> —Matthew 5:1

> Then the Lord said to Moses, "Come up to me on the mountain. Stay there, and I will give you the tablets of stone on which I have inscribed the instructions and commands so you can teach the people."
>
> —Exodus 24:12

1. Often when God wanted to give higher, more complete instruction, He invited His people to come up. Ask Holy Spirit to show you any place where you are sitting down in your comfort zone, refusing to come up higher to see what the Lord wants to show you.

> Everything is permissible for me, but not all things are beneficial. Everything is permissible for me, but I will not be enslaved by anything and brought under its power, allowing it to control me.
>
> —1 Corinthians 6:12

> You, my brothers and sisters, were called to be free. But do not use your freedom to indulge the flesh rather, serve one another humbly in love. For the entire law is fulfilled in keeping this one command: "Love your neighbor as yourself."
>
> —Galatians 5:13–14

2. Freedom doesn't mean we can live life selfishly doing only what we want. It means we are free from the power of sin so we can follow God's ways. Pray, asking God to show you what is in your heart about "commandments." As you reflect on Biblical commandments begin to ask God to show you any that prompt you to realize sin in your life.

> Search me, O God, and know my heart; Try
> me, and know my anxieties; And see if there is
> any wicked way in me, And lead me in the way
> everlasting.

3. God is not looking for ways to condemn us. He is
   looking for things that keep us away from His perfect
   plan and purpose for our lives. Praying these verses
   from a sincere heart, be willing to let go of the wicked
   and let Him lead you to His wonderful way.

THE TRUTH:
NOTHING BUT THE TRUTH

Today's culture is often referred to as the "post-truth" era. The media bombards the world with "fake" news. Social media provides a way for disinformation to seem like hard, cold facts. You may be living your life, going about normal things when a pop-up gives you something to worry about; some "breaking bombshell" rocks your peace. You may have trusted something an "expert" said a month ago, and now you are hearing that it was wrong. We don't know who in the world we can believe anymore. The truth is, there has never been anyone in the world we could believe to be 100% right 100% of the time. Except One.

Jesus said, *"I am the way, the truth, and the life. No one can come to the Father except through me. If you had really known me, you would know who my Father is. From now on, you do know him and have seen him!"* In this fallen world, the only source for truth is Our Father, Our Savior, and Holy Spirit who reveals it all to us.

One of the greatest attacks against truth in the world today is against The Bible. Many describe it as an ancient collection of wisdom writings and allegorical stories. For me, it was a lifeline that connected me to Jesus. It was alive and helped me understand why I knew everything in my life had changed, even before I saw some situations change. I began to search Scripture for the phrase "get up" which God spoke to me and found that He had spoken it to others. The more I studied the Bible, the more alive it became.

It is a supernatural book. People say that the Bible was written by about 40 different men from very different backgrounds across a span of about 1500 years. But it wasn't. It was written by God through those people across all those years. It is His autobiography; He wants us to know Him so we can know how much He loves us and wants to bring good into our lives.

The number of fulfilled prophecies alone have made me come to know this book had to be the inspired Word of God. There are at least forty-four prophecies written in the Old Testament, from Genesis through Malachi, which Jesus fulfilled while He was on earth. Imagine what it was like when God told Isaiah that a virgin would have a child over 700 years before it happened. There are over a thousand prophecies in the Bible because God is the one who holds time in His hand, and He is the only one who knows the end from the very beginning.

A second point of decision comes in the life of every believer. It did for me: I had decided to ask Jesus into my life as my savior, and constant companion; and then I had to decide if I would believe the Bible as the truth. I had to decide whether I would read it, meditate on it, and seek His guidance through it or not. The decision to believe and follow the Bible has made a huge difference in my life. There are times when I'm not sure if I understand it or not, so I ask Holy Spirit to help me, and I use study guides to understand the context. But even in those times, I keep getting into the Word, so the Word gets into me.

Freedom Exercise:
Read, Reflect, Record

> All Scripture is inspired by God and is useful to teach us what is true and to make us realize what is wrong in our lives. It corrects us when we are wrong and teaches us to do what is right. God uses it to prepare and equip his people to do every good work.
>
> —2 Timothy 3:16–17

1. Prayerfully ask God to show you any place in your heart where you are disbelieving that Scripture is true and truly from God. He wants to show you anything that is holding you back from what He has planned for you.

> For the word of God is alive and powerful. It is sharper than the sharpest two-edged sword, cutting between soul and spirit, between joint and marrow. It exposes our innermost thoughts and desires.
>
> —Hebrews 4:12

2. Ask Holy Spirit to show you anything in your soul; (your mind, emotions, and will) that needs to be guided by Scripture. Ask for specific Scriptures addressing each one that He calls to mind. Then spend time meditating on those.

> . . . My word that goes forth from My mouth shall not return to Me void, But it shall accomplish what I please, and it shall prosper in the thing for which I sent it.
>
> —Isaiah 55:11

3. Is there a time in your life when you trusted and believed a Scripture; did you believe it meant you would see a specific outcome in your life, but it didn't happen? If there is, spend time with the Lord about that situation. Seek Him openly and honestly about this. Some prompting questions may be:

    •   God, did I misunderstand what that Scripture meant?

    •   Where were You, Jesus, in this situation?

- Lord, I need Your help in understanding this. What do You want to say to me about this?

- Search me, Oh Lord, and show me any unhealed wound, root of bitterness, or lies about You or Your Word that I am holding in my heart.

- Will You help me heal those?

- Is Your Bible True? Can I believe it?

JESUS' COMMANDMENTS: GREATEST, GOLDEN, GUIDANCE

IF YOU ARE LIKE ME, WHEN YOU HEAR THE WORD commandment immediately you see the two stone tablets of ten laws given to Moses. Certainly, those ten are important to us all. Many additional laws were given to the Israelites in the Torah; actually, there were 613 recorded in the Old Testament. That is an overwhelming number of rules and regulations, and we know that not one person was ever able to keep them all perfectly. Until Jesus came that is.

Throughout His walk on earth, Jesus modeled for us how to walk as a Spirit-filled man and not sin. He is our example and His words on commandments give us great guidance on how to live our lives.

Matthew records a time when a lawyer asked Jesus, *"Which is the great commandment in the law?"*

Jesus answered, *"You shall love the LORD your God with all your heart, with all your soul, and with all your mind. This is the first and great commandment. And the second is like it: You shall love your neighbor as yourself. On these two commandments hang all the Law and the Prophets."*

Jesus further explained the second part, which has become the "Golden Rule," by saying, *"Do to others whatever you would like them to do to you. This is the essence of all that is taught in the law and the prophets.*

Jesus' ministry revealed His miraculous, supernatural power. However, He also shows us how practical and essential He is. Love, the complete, unrestrained love of God, is essential to our lives. If we don't love Him, we will never know Him, or have faith in Him or serve Him. Without love for Him, our souls will die, even if our bodies live on. Once we have that love connection with Him, His love will flow out from us into the world which desperately needs it.

He is also practical. Throughout His earthly ministry He "led the command" being formed to become the Spiritual Special Forces in God's kingdom. God the Father gave Him the authority to carry out His mission. Studying His words, I began to see the things He commanded to guide His "troops" so they could serve Him in the Kingdom.

My life has been greatly impacted by so many of them. Here are a few:

Seek His Kingdom

"Seek first the kingdom of God and His righteousness, and all these things shall be added to you."

—Matt. 6:33

When I focus on this uncertain world of brokenness and evil, I become a self-driven, fearful man. When I seek Him, He gives me peace because I know He is there and that His ways will lead me to all He has created for me. And, *He will keep those in perfect peace whose minds are stayed upon Him.* That is a promise I hold on to. You can do the same.

Judge Not

"Do not judge others, and you will not be judged. For you will be treated as you treat others. The standard you use in judging is the standard by which you will be judged."

—Matt. 7:1–2

I hope I never forget what a great gift my salvation is. How amazing that God reached down, touched the life of such a failure, and now calls me friend. As I deal with others, particularly hard to deal with people, I ask Holy Spirit to help me see the friend that is there inside them.

I'm so grateful that my sister looked at the deadbeat drugged-out person on her couch every day and judged me as a man worth saving. She judged my actions as wrong because she knew where they were leading me, but she never judged me as hopeless. She just kept pouring that water on me until I got up and came to know the living water.

Walk the Narrow Way

"Enter by the narrow gate; for wide is the gate and broad is the way that leads to destruction, and there are many who go in by it. Because narrow is the gate and difficult is the way which leads to life, and there are few who find it."

—Matt. 7:13–14

Angel and I lived a lot of our lives out there on the broad way. Our childhood was shaped and formed to a large degree because of people around us who lived out there, too. We loved the partying that went on, and we particularly enjoyed the alcohol.

As we have stepped into the kingdom, we know that we have been saved. But there has been a journey to be set free from the pull of the addiction to alcohol. Jesus wants us to be willing to shut the gate to the broad way. He can't deliver us until we lock the gate to the broad way. Our home is founded on the narrow way. Alcohol and all the things from the past are no longer welcome in our home.

Deny Yourself

"Then Jesus said to his disciples, 'If any of you wants to be my follower, you must give up your own way, take up your cross, and follow me. If you try to hang on to your life, you will lose it. But if you give up your life for my sake, you will save it. And what do you benefit if you gain the whole world but lose your own soul? Is anything worth more than your soul? For the Son of Man will come with his angels in the glory of his Father and will judge all people according to their deeds.'"

—Matthew 16:24–27

Serving in the military shed understanding for me into what Jesus meant in this Scripture. Basic training was full of challenges as I learned that I needed to follow the commands given to me. Often, I failed and was given many chances to practice push-ups as punishment until I learned. Over time, however, the discipline helped me grow stronger and be more effective as I served. I can't imagine what would have happened if I had decided to just do what I wanted during deployment, instead of following our leadership. They had intel we knew nothing about and knew what needed to be done, and when to do it, so that we safely accomplished our mission.

Now that I am in the Spiritual Special Forces there is so much more riding on the mission Jesus has for us. When Holy Spirit tells us to reach out to someone, it's because

He knows the condition of their soul. An encounter with us may be the only touch from God they received that day. Particularly in these uncertain days, it may be a critical time in their life. I want to take up my cross daily because I don't want to stand before Jesus one day and acknowledge that I decided to do what I wanted to do and missed a chance to tell a lost soul about Him. I love Him too much to want to do that.

Make Disciples

"Go and make disciples of all the nations, baptizing them in the name of the Father and the Son and the Holy Spirit. Teach these new disciples to obey all the commands I have given you. And be sure of this: I am with you always, even to the end of the age."

—Matt. 28:19–20

Christians call this the Great Commission because it is conveying the words of the risen Christ to the eleven disciples as He gave them instructions on how to continue His ministry. Two words there caught my attention. The first is "go"; it comes from the Greek word that can be translated "as you are going". The second is "nations" which in Greek is "ethnos." This Scripture certainly encourages the Church to send missions into all the world to disciple those who hear the Gospel of Jesus and are converted. However, this also means that as I am going about my everyday life, I should share the Gospel with those on my path and be ready to encourage them into a relationship with Jesus and become disciples. When we do that, we will be part of recruiting more boots, or maybe sandals, on the ground in the kingdom.

Freedom Exercise:
Read, Reflect, Record

> "If you love Me, keep My commandments. And I will pray the Father, and He will give you another Helper, that He may abide with you forever—the Spirit of truth, whom the world cannot receive, because it neither sees Him nor knows Him; but you know Him, for He dwells with you and will be in you. "
>
> —John 14: 15–17

1. Jesus used commandments to give us guidance on how to live Kingdom lives. However, He didn't *demand* we do things. Reflect on the Scriptures from the paragraphs above and these verses from John 14.

2. Ask Holy Spirit which guidance from Jesus needs your attention in your life right now.

3. As you read and study your Bible, ask Holy Spirit to highlight additional guidance commandments from Jesus. Open your heart and let the love you feel for your Savior motivate you to follow that guidance.

IF:
THE MOST POWERFUL
TWO-LETTER WORD IN THE BIBLE

JESUS MADE A WAY FOR US TO LIVE THE ABUNDANT, joyful life God the Father intended us to have. When we are saved, we are sealed by Holy Spirit, and will one day live with Jesus in Heaven for all eternity. Jesus paid for us to have that privilege; but He didn't intend for us to continue in our broken, empty lives until they end, and we go to heaven. But just as he let the rich young ruler walk away from living the kingdom life, He will let us choose that too. He will allow us to walk away sad.

He shows us that we have a choice by the frequent use of the word *if*. The first place I noticed it was in Jeremiah 29. The well-known Scripture tells us that God has a plan to give us a future and a hope and bring us peace, not evil. Then His Word tells us we will find Him and His plan for us when we seek for Him with all our heart. There must come that "when" for us to find Him—if we don't seek Him with *all* our heart, we will miss the wonderful things He has planned for us.

The Hebrew word translated as heart is "lebab," which means *the inner man.* Our inner man means our mind, our emotion, and our will.

When I was living life in the old ways, I produced only rotten fruit. I belittled my kids and intimidated them, so I produced broken relationships with them. I was so angry and critical of my wife I produced hopelessness in her heart, and at times, she became suicidal.

As I sought to be close to Jesus by reading His words and understanding His ways, I began to see dark places in my heart; places where fear and control issues lived; places where I wanted only my way; places where I needed to "get up" and look for Him.

My stepson Mason and I had a very troubled relationship for many years. He had started getting into trouble when he was thirteen and I formed many judgments against him over the years. When I was in San Antonio, Texas recovering from the gunshot wound, I needed a full-time caregiver. Of all the people He could have picked, God told Angel that Mason was the person for the job. We were going to be living in a tiny hotel-sized room together 24/7. I was not happy about that, in fact, I was totally against that idea.

Mason learned how to take care of me physically and he did it very well. He never brought up anything from the past and he extended grace and mercy to me as he cared for my wounds. During our days together, God began to take care of what was abiding in my heart about Mason. The desire of my heart was for our family to be unified and loving. I could not hold on to the judgmental criticism I had about Mason and expect God to be able to help me fulfill that desire.

As I prayed often and let Holy Spirit highlight God's Word to me, the anger and animosity I felt toward Mason left my heart. All the blaming I had done in my mind toward Mason was replaced by seeing the blessings he brought to my life. I was humbled by Mason and the way he cared for me and was filled with gratitude for him. Through that journey, he became my best friend and beloved son. The healing of that relationship opened the way for Jesus to heal our family. Jesus put me in an undesirable situation so He could give me the desire of my heart. The only thing standing between a healthy family and me was the powerful little word *if*.

Freedom Exercise:
Read, Reflect, Record

> "I am the vine; you are the branches. He who abides in Me, and I in him, bears much fruit; for without Me you can do nothing. If you abide in Me, and My words abide in you, you will ask what you desire, and it shall be done for you.
>
> —John 15:5,7

1. Read and reflect on these verses. Sit in the Presence of the Lord and consider the desire of your heart.

2. Prayerfully ask Holy Spirit to show you where in your heart (thoughts, emotions, and will) you are not letting Jesus abide; where are you shutting Him out?

3. Spend time praying for Jesus to come into those places; give Him permission to come and live there. As you go about your day, raise your awareness of Him in all the minutes of your life. Are there any judgments against others you are holding on to? Ask Jesus to help you release those and tell you how He sees those people.

4. If you want a deeper look into this, take some time
    to read through your Bible, highlighting the "if"
    Scriptures.

REAL POWER

As a U.S. Army Green Beret, I was always focused on working out and conditioning my muscles. There were many repetitions of each exercise required to make any real progress. If I wanted to have bigger, stronger biceps I had to focus on bicep curls, rows, and chin-ups. Interestingly, however, the most powerful and deadly muscle we have in our body is our tongue. Scripture tells us that death and life are in the power of the tongue.

We can speak words of pain and suffering to those around us when all we do is criticize and put them down. Think about some you may have heard; *that'll never work, you can't do that, you will never succeed, you always mess things up, etc.* Think about the phrases we use to describe hurtful words; *biting remarks, sharp words, cut to the core.* All of those form a mental picture of inflicting painful wounds.

Or we can speak powerful encouragement to other people when we see their good qualities and praise them. When we call out the God-given qualities we know are in a person, it helps them believe in themselves and begin to see who they truly are. If we praise someone's creativity it encourages them to create. Praise for someone's abilities helps them want to get even better. When we lift others up, it is like a breath of fresh air; literally, it breathes life into them.

I have to ask myself a question about the people I am in a relationship with; "Am I going to agree with the devil about them, or am I going to agree with what Jesus says about them?" It doesn't mean I can't talk with them about hard situations we may be going through when we see things differently. It just means that I will always agree with God about who they are and who He is growing them to be. That is crucial in finding better ways of relating to each other.

We can also speak death or life into our situations. Some generational curses are carried forward by speaking them over ourselves. If all your ancestors were poor, and you keep saying that you are poor because your family has always been poor, then you are believing and giving life to staying in a poverty mentality. You will be so focused on your lack; you may miss many opportunities from God who is trying to bring financial success into your life. People do this over diseases, addictions, intelligence, and careers. I definitely had a "failure" belief over myself and spoke about it frequently. They had to give me a "social promotion" to get me out of middle school. I spoke death into every opportunity to learn that came my way. That is until God began to work in my soul. He changed the way my heart believed about myself. If He thought I was worth saving, shouldn't I believe in me, too?

The repetition of our tongue for negative, critical statements kills off what God is doing in our life. The repetition of our tongue for Truth brings about our True Life. The most frequent attack of the enemy of our soul is against the Word of God. Remember in Eden the devil said to Eve, *Did God really say that you must not eat of every tree in the garden?* Listening to that snake caused her to fall and to lose the life God had planned for her and her family. He still wants to slither up to us today and do the same thing. He wants to tell me I'm not worthy to step on a speaking platform, that I'm not good enough, etc. But I stay ready for the battle and say, "This is what My Savior says, *'I have sent him out to proclaim the kingdom of God!* and, *"As the Father has sent Me, I also send you."* There is the power of life in those statements.

**Freedom Exercise
Read, Reflect, Record**

> A man's stomach will be filled with the fruit of his mouth. He will be filled with what his lips speak. Death and life are in the power of the tongue, and those who love it will eat its fruit.
>
> —Proverbs 18:20–21

1. Prayerfully ask Holy Spirit to show you what is coming out of your mouth. Are you speaking death over people, yourself, and situations? Or are you speaking life?

> Things which proceed out of the mouth come from the heart, and they defile a man.
>
> —Matthew 15:18

2. Jesus says that what is in our heart is what comes out of our mouth. Ask Holy Spirit to show you things that have come out of your mouth that you would never have wanted to say in front of Jesus. As these things

come to mind, confess them to Jesus and ask for His forgiveness.

Then ask Holy Spirit to show you what you are holding in your heart that causes you to say what you did. You may find some unhealed hurts, some lies about others that you have turned into the truth about them, or maybe some fear. Whatever it is, Holy Spirit wants to comfort and heal and cleanse you from all of it. Invite Holy Spirit in to do His transforming work.

> The tongue is also a small part of the body, but it can speak big things. See how a very small fire can set many trees on fire.
>
> —James 3:5

3. Spend time in prayer asking Jesus to show you anywhere there is a scorched ruin that you set in place by your words. Ask Him to help you have the courage to go to those you have hurt and make amends, offer acts of repentance, and express the sorrow you feel about the hurt your words caused.

> If a person thinks he is religious, but does not keep his tongue from speaking bad things, he is fooling himself. His religion is worth nothing.
>
> —James 1: 26

4. Our Lord's brother is teaching us to not be like the Scribes and Pharisees who were self-righteous and religious but didn't have a close personal relationship with Jesus. If our talk is criticizing, tearing down, negative, and judgmental, now is a good time to take stock of that. Holy Spirit will lead you into all truth; all you have to do is ask.

†††

PART 3

REACH UP!

Who is the King of glory?
The LORD of Heaven's Armies.
He is the King of glory.

—Psalm 24:10

HIGHER WAYS

IT IS MEDICALLY IMPOSSIBLE FOR A VOICE BOX, shattered by a .45 caliber bullet, to begin functioning again. Medical experts will tell you that if you lose over 40 percent of your blood you will go into hemorrhagic shock; and if you lose 50 percent, your heart can no longer pump blood. When a bullet rips into a human shoulder and arm nerve bundle, medical specialists know there will be a loss of function to the arm.

It is scientifically impossible for me to lose 75 percent of my blood and be alive; scientifically impossible for me to speak, scientifically impossible for me to use my right arm. But God made it all possible

I have come to know and serve a God who defies the natural, scientific world we live in so His Kingdom purposes will be accomplished. It is scientifically impossible for a man to walk on water, for a bush to burn without burning up, for a virgin to conceive a child, for a man to live inside a fish for three days, for leprosy to be healed at the touch of a man, for a dead man to come back to life and walk out of a tomb. But God caused all these things to happen and be recorded in the Holy Scriptures so we could know His greatness. God is not bound by the limited scientific understanding of man.

God is so much more than we can even begin to understand. *He made the world and everything in it, since He is Lord of heaven and earth, and does not dwell in temples made with hands.* Amazingly, God's greatest desire is for us to seek Him out and come to know Him. God gave Isaiah a vision so we could begin to see His glory as He recorded, "*I saw the Lord sitting on a throne, high and lifted up, and the train of His robe filled the temple.* The more we seek to know Him, the more aware we become of how great and glorious He truly is.

When God showed Isaiah his glory, it made him realize what a sinful man he was. In the moment of that realization, God sent an angel to touch Isaiah's lips and purge his sin. When Isaiah saw His glory, then confessed and was cleansed of sin, God was able to use him. So, He asked, "*Whom shall I send, and who will go for Us?*" Scripture records Isaiah's immediate response, "*Here am I! Send me.*"

Here am I, living a scientifically impossible life, because a God that is exceedingly abundantly more than I can even imagine told me to Get Up! Jesus came into my life bringing forgiveness for my sins and restoration for my life. How could I not answer with Isaiah, "*Here am I! Send me!*"

Freedom Exercise:
Read, Reflect, Record

> Yours, O Lord, is the greatness, the power, the glory, the victory, and the majesty. Everything in the heavens and on earth is yours, O Lord, and this is your kingdom. We adore you as the one who is over all things. Wealth and honor come from you alone, for you rule over everything. Power and might are in your hand, and at your discretion people are made great and given strength.
>
> —1 Chronicles 29: 11–12

1. Prayerfully read these verses and meditate on the majesty of God. As you do, set aside any preconceived notions, or limitations you have about Him and ask Holy Spirit to allow you to see beyond the physical into the heavens.

> Now when evening came, the boat was in the middle of the sea; and He was alone on the land. Then He saw them straining at rowing, for the

wind was against them. Now about the fourth watch of the night He came to them, walking on the sea, and would have passed them by. And when they saw Him walking on the sea, they supposed it was a ghost, and cried out; for they all saw Him and were troubled. But immediately He talked with them and said to them, "Be of good cheer! It is I; do not be afraid." Then He went up into the boat to them, and the wind ceased. And they were greatly amazed in themselves beyond measure, and marveled.

—Mark 6:47–51

2. Let these verses remind you of a time when Jesus supernaturally came into your life and brought salvation to you. Prayerfully ask Holy Spirit to refresh the amazement and wonder you felt; spend time praising Jesus for what He has done and for who He is in your life.

3. Search your heart to find how you would answer God's question, *Whom shall I send, and who will go for Us?*

WE NEED TO TALK

Some of my earliest memories include the image of my grandma, Rosie, on her knees praying for her family. She was praying for us all to come to know Jesus. I didn't understand her faith during that part of my life, but I believe that she was planting seeds that would prepare my heart to one day personally know Jesus.

That image of my grandmother has become an icon for faith that is deep in my heart. To ever truly Get Up, we need to get down on our knees. We are approaching a Holy God, the creator of the universe, the King of Glory. Kneeling before Him is acknowledging His greatness, and our wonder at His presence with us. Our model of how to walk on earth as a spirit-filled man, Jesus, did this often; He did it reverently and He did it in solitude. His words tell us that He never did anything His Father didn't tell Him to do, and He never said anything His Father didn't tell Him to say. He talked and listened to His Father.

Nothing in my earthly history taught me how to be a son of God, how to walk in the kingdom, how to be a godly husband or father, or how to live a kingdom life.

I now read the Bible and I am grateful that it gives me great understanding. However, life around me is fast-paced and sometimes confusing, so I just need to talk to my Father about things. I need to sit at His feet and let Him love on me and give me wisdom. I need to start my day with His voice in my heart and head and end my day resting in His grace and mercy.

He spoke to me while there were flying bullets and chaos all around me. So, I know He is always there to talk to us and listen to us. Scripture tells us that we are to pray without ceasing. I've come to understand that there can be a constant communication between God and me. So, as I go about my day, I can talk to God and hear from Him. That doesn't mean that I have to stop what I am doing and go away from everybody and kneel down. But that image of kneeling before Him represents the position of my heart; it is what I reflect in my attitude toward him as I talk to Him throughout my day.

Reading in 1 Peter 2 we find a beautiful picture of who we are in Christ, "*You are coming to Christ, who is the living cornerstone of God's temple. He was rejected by people, but he was chosen by God for great honor. And you are living stones that God is building into his spiritual temple. What's more, you are his holy priests.*"

That Scripture calls to mind what Jesus said in the middle of cleansing the temple. He was turning over tables and chairs and setting things right. He quotes from Isaiah and says, *"My house will be a house of prayer."* In that moment He was talking about the physical temple; however, the Word tells us we are His spiritual temple. We too, are to be a "house of prayer". Only through our connection to Him, will we be aware of the things that need to be overturned, the things that are robbing us of the right use of our lives.

When I look at the Isaiah verses Jesus quoted in the temple that day, I find a deep message for us all. There we find why the Father wants us to be in prayer with Him, *I will bring them to my holy mountain of Jerusalem and will fill them with joy in my house of prayer.* I can hear the voice of my Father saying, "Son, do you want more joy in your life? Come, let's talk about it."

Freedom Exercise: Read, Reflect, Record

> Hear me as I pray, O Lord. Be merciful and answer me! My heart has heard you say, "Come and talk with me." And my heart responds, "Lord, I am coming."
>
> —Psalm 27:7–8

1. Use these verses as you pray. Let your response truly be from your heart. Focus on the "talk with me" portion. A good conversation with God includes being sure to listen. Sometimes His children need to sit in silence and wait to hear from Him.

    > I love the Lord because he hears my voice and my prayer for mercy. Because he bends down to listen, I will pray as long as I have breath!
    >
    > —Psalm 116:1–2

2. As you meditate on these verses, let an image of you kneeling in supplication before Him come into your mind and heart. See your Father bending down to you. He's listening; what do you truly desire to say to Him?

> Therefore, put on every piece of God's armor so you will be able to resist the enemy in the time of evil. Then after the battle you will still be standing firm. Stand your ground, putting on the belt of truth and the body armor of God's righteousness. For shoes, put on the peace that comes from the Good News so that you will be fully prepared. In addition to all of these, hold up the shield of faith to stop the fiery arrows of the devil. Put on salvation as your helmet, and take the sword of the Spirit, which is the word of God.
>
> Pray in the Spirit at all times and on every occasion. Stay alert and be persistent in your prayers for all believers everywhere.
>
> —Ephesians 6:13–18

3. These are the verses of instruction for when we come under attack from the enemy. Pray through this Scripture paying close attention to the last two lines. Ask Holy Spirit to show you how to increase your constant communication with God; He wants us to participate with Him to gain the victory He has won for us.

PASSOVER

When Angel and I wrote the first book, our publisher had the cover created by a gifted graphic designer. Working from the manuscript, she added a red streak across the top. That element was placed there because people who saw me after I was shot, at first thought the blood pouring from my throat was a red scarf. A little while after the book was released Jesus impressed on my heart that the streak represented the Passover.

As I began to pray and seek a greater understanding about that, it became very clear. I was living in exactly what Egypt symbolized for the Israelites. The world around me was holding me captive to sin and my life was becoming harder and harder. When God began to open the way to free His children, He asked them to put the blood of the lamb on their doorpost to keep the angel of death away from them. When I was laying on the ground bleeding out and calling out for Jesus, I was calling on the power and protection by the Blood of Jesus, the Lamb of God. God heard my whispered cry and death was defeated.

The journey of the Israelites reveals that God sent Moses to Pharoah eight times to tell him to "Let My people go!" That encourages me to know that whatever it takes, God will keep working with us to set us free. The number seven represents perfection or completeness. When we see the number eight, it means longer than it had to be. Sometimes we can see that throughout our lives, the "plagues" have to keep getting worse, we have to keep getting closer to the very bottom of our lives, and devastation must be close at hand before we Get Up, claim our freedom, and follow God into our promised land.

He equips us with everything we need to make it through the journey to living free. As God's children went toward the promised land, they met a big challenge—the Red Sea in front and the Egyptians chasing after them! The people cried out to Moses, and he told them to stand firm because God would fight their battle. And the Lord said to Moses, *"Why do you cry to Me? Tell the children of Israel to go forward. But lift up your rod and stretch out your hand over the sea and divide it. And the children of Israel shall go on dry ground through the midst of the sea."*

God did His part. He always does. But we must be willing to claim the power, the authority, and the skills and talents He has made available to us to participate with Him in the victory.

Jesus became the perfect lamb who was sacrificed to pay the atonement for our lives. He made the way for us to become children of God. With the first drop of blood from that cross, we were granted redemption and were made ready to serve Jesus. He said, *"I have been given all authority in heaven and on earth."* He is the source of everything we need to live free. He is also the source of everything we need to minister in His name, *He called his twelve disciples together, and gave them power and authority over all devils, and to cure diseases. And he sent them to preach the kingdom of God, and to heal the sick."*

With Jesus as our Savior, we pass over out of death into the life He purposed and planned for us. He did His part, and I don't know about you, but I don't want to miss a bit of what He has planned for me. So, I will keep getting up and following Him!

Freedom Exercise:
Read, Reflect, Record

As Pharaoh approached, the people of Israel looked up and panicked when they saw the Egyptians overtaking them. They cried out to the Lord, and they said to Moses, "Why did you bring us out here to die in the wilderness? Weren't there enough graves for us in Egypt? What have you done to us? Why did you make us leave Egypt? Didn't we tell you this would happen while we were still in Egypt? We said, 'Leave us alone! Let us be slaves to the Egyptians. It's better to be a slave in Egypt than a corpse in the wilderness!'"

But Moses told the people, "Don't be afraid. Just stand still and watch the Lord rescue you today. The Egyptians you see today will never be seen again. The Lord himself will fight for you. Just stay calm."

Then the Lord said to Moses, "Why are you crying out to me? Tell the people to get moving! Pick up your staff and raise your hand over the sea. Divide the water so the Israelites can walk through the middle of the sea on dry ground.

—Exodus 14:10–16

1. Prayerfully read these verses. Ask Holy Spirit to call to mind any time when you started following the Lord but wanted to turn back. What does Jesus want to say to you about that time? If you did turn aside, open your heart, and talk to Holy Spirit about what happened. Ask to see that situation the way Jesus saw it.

2. God has equipped us all to participate with Him in gaining our freedom. Reflect on the talents, skills, and abilities God has given you. If you aren't aware of these, ask Holy Spirit to show you. God wants to give you all you need; don't hesitate to ask for what He has for you.

> In his grace, God has given us different gifts for doing certain things well. So, if God has given you the ability to prophesy, speak out with as much faith as God has given you. If your gift is serving others, serve them well. If you are a teacher, teach well. If your gift is to encourage others, be encouraging. If it is giving, give generously. If God has given you leadership ability, take the responsibility seriously. And if you have a gift for showing kindness to others, do it gladly.
>
> —Romans 12 6–8

Note: For additional words on spiritual gifts see
1 Corinthians 12:4–11 and 12:28

3. The above verses, and those in 1 Corinthians, encourage us to participate in kingdom work as God has equipped us to do. Ask Jesus to show you how He sees your spiritual gifting and for revelation to see where you are to use them.

GOD'S FAVORITES

ANGEL AND I TELL THE STORY OF WHAT HAS happened in our lives since God has shown up so that we can encourage others to see God in their situations and lives. We want people to know how much God loves them. We see so much more now than we ever saw or understood about God. We have been witnesses to His power to save both spiritually and physically. Our relationships with each other, family, and friends have radically changed. This journey has been humbling and amazing. Neither of us earned the privilege of being saved by Him. When we look at the quality of our lives before Him, we marvel at His mercy and His grace. We know that He gave us the worthiest gift of all when there was nothing in our lives worthy of that gift. He wants to give that gift to every single person ever created.

The Word tells us that God is no respecter of people; He loves us all and wants to have a relationship with each one of us.

Peter's encounter with Cornelius is a great illustration of how God wants to make sure we understand that. When

Peter was very hungry God gave him a vision of all types of food; then He told him to get up, kill it and eat it. Peter was appalled because all of it was "unclean" according to Jewish traditions. Peter declared his great religious perfection, saying he wouldn't eat it. God, however, said that He had made it clean and told Peter, "*What God has made clean, do not call common.*"

God had also sent an angel to tell Cornelius to send and ask Peter to come to his house. The Gentile men he sent arrived at Peter's house just as he was pondering the meaning of the vision. God told him to go with them because Cornelius and other Gentiles wanted to know the good news.

God is involved in every detail of our lives; He isn't limited by distance and man-made divisions. He moves in the world to show us He doesn't have favorites. Peter thought he was set apart by his religion; he wasn't, and neither are we. Peter thought that Cornelius and all like him were "unclean" in God's sight so he shouldn't have anything to do with him. He would never have gone with those Gentile men without God's prompting.

I know that God could have told Cornelius the good news through the angel He had sent to him. However, He sent Peter to go and tell him. God wants to use all of us to carry forth the message He has for the world. He doesn't want any distance between His children. He created one race, the human race, full of unique expressions of His creation. All of us who believe in Jesus and have received Him into our hearts and lives have life through one blood; His blood shed on Calvary for all sins. We are all invited to live together in unity in one eternal amazing kingdom where we are all His favorites.

Freedom Exercise:
Read, Reflect, Record

> Peter told them, "You know it is against our laws
> for a Jewish man to enter a Gentile home like
> this or to associate with you. But God has shown
> me that I should no longer think of anyone as
> impure or unclean.

> —Acts 10:28

1. As you pray today, ask Holy Spirit to show you where
   the world has taught you division between you and
   others. As you reflect, consider race, age, denominations,
   political views, nations, and other divisions that may be
   in your soul. Ask what God wants to show you today.

> Jesus replied, "I assure you, no one can enter
> the Kingdom of God without being born of
> water and the Spirit. Humans can reproduce
> only human life, but the Holy Spirit gives birth
> to spiritual life. So don't be surprised when I say,
> 'You must be born again.'

> —John 3:5–7

> "For this is how God loved the world: He gave his one and only Son, so that everyone who believes in him will not perish but have eternal life. God sent his Son into the world not to judge the world, but to save the world through him.
>
> —John 3: 16–17

2. These verses from John 3 are Jesus' instructions for us about how to be saved and live in the Kingdom of God. Ask Holy Spirit to show you what you need to see about your kingdom life.

    Have you fully believed that He has made you clean; is there anything you think you can't be forgiven for? Is there guilt that you still carry in your heart? Ask Holy Spirit to remove it so you can receive the grace Jesus paid so high a price to give you.

    Have you truly been born again; or are you walking only in religious doctrine to try to walk a kingdom life? Allow Holy Spirit to work in your soul today, filling you with spiritual life.

PART 4

ALL THINGS NEW

*If anyone is in Christ, the new creation has come:
The old has gone, the new is here!*

—2 Corinthians 5:17

COCOONED IN DARKNESS

A HOME IS INTENDED TO BE A SAFE PLACE WHERE children can have time to grow and discover who they are and live happy lives. I grew up in Battle Creek, Michigan, and my home was a battleground where I experienced anger, rejection, and physical abuse from my mother. It was impossible to escape the realization that of her four children, I was the only one she seemed to hate. Because of my mother's struggles, my childhood experiences wrapped my heart and mind with continuing darkness. Every time she verbally abused me, called me names, and shamed me, there was a layer of darkness added. Another layer was added when she physically attacked me. Still more darkness came when I saw her show love for my siblings as she ridiculed me.

With every layer of darkness, my heart became increasingly empty and cold. Responding to a slight glimmer which I thought to be love, I started dating a young man when I was seventeen and married him at twenty-one, in an attempt to fill that empty place. Six years and two children later, I realized he was faithfully married to his addition to narcotics: but not to me.

The path I thought would lead to happiness only led me deeper into darkness. This path was a dead-end for me. I was broken and lonely, divorced, working two jobs, caring for two children, and completely overwhelmed with the pressure of just trying to hold it all together. I finally concluded that my existence was not life. I made several attempts to kill myself; to stop acting like I was alive when I knew I wasn't. I was so wrapped in darkness I thought I was darkness.

I look back at my life as I stood near death's door and can see that God intervened and kept me alive. When I realize that, I am humbled. I had nothing to offer anyone, particularly God; yet He saved my life.

Intense professional counseling helped me overcome the desire to end my life. But that alone could not pierce the darkness in my soul. It did, however, help me find my way in the darkness.

A decade later I met John and we made a heart connection at the place where I was desperate to love and be loved. He was my friend, my confidant, and the love of my life. His love for me began to lift the darkness. I loved him even when our journey was not smooth. I loved him when he was deployed and through everything we experienced with our kids and family. The love John and I shared was the first light in my life.

Freedom Exercise:
Read, Reflect, Record

> For this reason, I bow my knees and pray to the Father. It is from Him that every family in heaven and on earth has its name. I pray that because of the riches of His shining-greatness, He will make you strong with power in your hearts through the Holy Spirit. I pray that Christ may live in your hearts by faith. I pray that you will be filled with love. I pray that you will be able to understand how wide and how long and how high and how deep His love is. I pray that you will know the love of Christ. His love goes beyond anything we can understand. I pray that you will be filled with God Himself.
>
> —Ephesians 3:14–19

1. As you pray today, join your heart with the apostle Paul's prayer, pray it over yourself, and for others that are in your heart.

2. Reflect on anything that stirs your Spirit; ask Holy Spirit for clarity.

> Now to Him who is able to do exceedingly abundantly above all that we ask or think, according to the power that works in us, to Him be glory in the church by Christ Jesus to all generations, forever and ever. Amen.
>
> —Ephesians 3:20–21

3. Paul's prayer is for all generations to see God's glory. Pray for the legacy that God has for you to come forth into your generations and glorify Him.

BEING BORN

With John in my life, I was able to face a situation that brought intense pain, sadness, and darkness that could have overcome me. John being with me carried me through, and together we saw a miracle.

My dad was my rock and a loving parent to all of us. He loved to take us into the woods and share his love for the outdoors. A great weekend he spent with my brother, Robert, ended in unspeakable tragedy. They had both been so excited about going to the woods and getting to hunt together. Robert bought a new truck, and they both bought new rifles. The day they were heading out to hunt, my dad laid his gun down in the bed of the truck and it discharged just as my brother walked into the line of fire. My brother's last words, "I'm hit," pierced my dad's heart because it was his gun that caused his death.

Losing my brother was like losing a part of me. He knew me, my history, my journey. We had shared life in a family. It was no accident that God had made him my brother. But it was a tragic accident that took him away. There was a black hole in the middle of my heart where my brother's friendship had been. Where was God when that gun went off?

I asked God that question. I asked it in my angriest voice out of a place where I knew He could have stopped it, but He hadn't. I asked it because I wanted Him to tell me He was sorry for not stopping this awful thing from happening. I asked it, not wanting Him to explain; I just wanted my brother back! I was angry and I let Him know it.

Gently, over time, He began to help me see all that happened as a part of His plan. He didn't cause the gun to go off. He knew that was coming though and used that awful tragedy for good. We found out that my brother accepted Jesus 10 days before the accident. I began to realize all the people and situations in my brother's life that God used to soften his heart and get him to come to know Jesus. God was aware that the gun would discharge, so Holy Spirit made a way for my brother to come to faith before that day. God wanted all my family to be saved, so not only was my brother saved, but God used his death to move my dad, my mom, and me into His hands too.

When Christ came into my family, everything began to change. There was a definite change in my mother. Always before when I was near her, I sensed she viewed me as a threat. Now that atmosphere around her was gone. It took us time as we worked through all the pain that we had brought to each other. But God kept guiding us toward reconciliation. Part of my darkness was because of the pain from unhealed hurts because of my mother's alcoholism. Mental and emotional pain is not something you can easily process in the world. If you say your head hurts, someone will offer you an aspirin. But if you say your heart hurts, no one knows what to offer you except sympathy; and that just brings more pain.

One of the heaviest parts of my darkness was lifted off when she came to me and apologized for being the kind of mother she had been to me. Hearing her acknowledge that she had been wrong, helped me tremendously. She was sincere and I offered her my forgiveness. It also prompted me to apologize and ask her to forgive me for the times that I reacted in anger and for the things I had done in revenge. Admitting my part of the ongoing abuse and anger broke the destructive cycle and stopped the pain. We were finally at a place of peace with one another. She began to tell me she loved me every time I left one of our visits, and I began to believe her.

When that piece of darkness lifted, it took with it the oppression that happens when we think we are not just unloved, but that we are *unlovable*. She had not loved me well over the years, but she had loved me with all the love she had to give. Having Jesus in her heart gave her true love to give. When she gave me that love, it flooded the empty places in my soul and fed the growth of my true self.

The timing of everything became so clear when my father was diagnosed with cancer a year after he had been saved. God knew that was coming, too. My dad's newly found faith and love of Jesus gave him a great hunger for the Word of God. The Bible strengthened and encouraged him in all the days he was dealing with cancer and treatments and bouts of being so sick.

While my dad was getting sicker and weaker, he had to deal with the unexpected death of my mother. She died of a sudden aneurism. He was barely able to go to her funeral, but God helped him through it. His last good-bye to her was said when he saw her resting in the peace of the Lord, and my dad marveled at how beautiful she was. It helped me see the love my dad felt for her, and I was grateful God had given him that opportunity. As hard as his journey through those days was, it was so much better because He had Jesus through it all.

After I realized that God's ways aren't my ways, but are so much higher than I can see, I went to Him and apologized for being so angry with Him. He met me with immediate forgiveness and filled me with His presence and the power of His love in my heart. The beautiful me that had been hidden inside the darkness grew in the presence of His grace.

Freedom Exercise:
Read, Reflect, Record

"He has delivered us from the power of darkness and conveyed us into the kingdom of the Son of His love, in whom we have redemption through His blood, the forgiveness of sins."

—Colossians 1:13–14

"If we confess our sins, he is faithful and just to forgive us our sins and to cleanse us from all unrighteousness."

—1 John 1:9

"For if you forgive other people when they sin against you, your heavenly Father will also forgive you."

—Matthew 6:14

1. Meditate on these verses; as you do, ask Holy Spirit to bring to mind any person you haven't forgiven.

2. If you become aware of unconfessed sin, confess it today. There is freedom in receiving forgiveness and in giving it. Forgiveness brings us closer to Jesus, who made the way for us to be forgiven.

> So from now on, we do not think about what people are like by looking at them. For if a man belongs to Christ, he is a new person. The old life is gone. New life has begun. All this comes from God. He is the One Who brought us to Himself when we hated Him. He did this through Christ. Then He gave us the work of bringing others to Him. God was in Christ. He was working through Christ to bring the whole world back to Himself. God no longer held men's sins against them. And He gave us the work of telling and showing people this.
>
> —2 Corinthians 5:16–16

3. Spend time today letting the Lord search your heart. Are you reconciled to Him and to other people? Ask if Jesus wants you to go and tell the power of reconciliation to someone in your life. Also, ask where you are to be a minister of reconciliation with someone.

4. Even in his death, the spiritual power that was in Angel's brother, touched her father's heart and then spread into the family. Invite Holy Spirit to stir to its fullest the power that is in you, asking for directions for sharing it with everyone around you.

LIGHT FOR THE DARKEST DAYS

THE TIME LEADING UP TO APRIL 2, 2014, HAD been defined by dealing with death in my family. Like all things, healing from the passing of a loved one is a process. Grief came in waves. Life went on, but some days I wasn't fully on board. However, I remembered the good things God had shown me and He kept prompting me to know His presence and accept His healing.

The move to Texas brought hope because it looked brand new! There was a new job I loved, new connections with some great people from the church, and a new start in my marriage. I was sure this state of wide-open spaces and sunlight would surely put an end to the last of the dark strongholds that still hid in my heart.

On that April day, I had just gotten home from work and was getting dinner ready for us when John's commanding officer came to the door to tell me my husband had been shot. Fear shooting through every cell of my body ushered in the darkness that had been waiting to be set free in my heart again. Was this the moment death was coming to finish its work in my heart and family?

However, God's presence was the power within me in that moment. Because He is greater than any fear, any darkness, any pain that comes our way, He moved in my spirit and I knew it was Him, not death, who had claimed my husband that day. My soul came alive with my shouted, "Thank You, God!"

God knew that without John, the darkness would fill me again. Our Father moved in my spirit when John was shot to keep me calm and remove my fear. Knowing that He was there with me encouraged me to be the person he planned me to be. His injury was so massive and hard to take in that occasionally, the brilliance of life stopped for a moment and my thought was, "This is just a dream!" Some days I walked around in a daze. God, however, never left me.

When I first walked into John's intensive care unit room and saw him, I totally lost it. It was overwhelming to see him on the bed with all kinds of tubes coming from him. His head was swollen as big as a basketball, which caused his tongue to stick out. I was devastated to see my husband so critically wounded by such a senseless act of violence. But God kept letting me know He was there with John and with me.

After the surgery, his doctor put him in a medically induced coma to give his body the complete rest it needed so he could heal. I sat down next to him, grasped his hand, and started telling him how much I loved him. He instantly responded, his eyes flew open, and he looked directly at me. The doctors quickly came into the room and got him back "under," but that moment helped my heart so much. I needed to see my husband respond to the love I was feeling for him. It helped sustain me for the long days ahead during his recovery.

It was years later before I could see God was leading us down the path to Spiritual transformation while we were on that road to recovery.

Freedom Exercise:
Read, Reflect, Record

> ". . . Now repent of your sins and turn to God, so that your sins may be wiped away. Then times of refreshment will come from the presence of the Lord."
>
> —Acts 3:19

1. These verses from Acts 3 reassure us that with the turning to God we can have a closeness with God. In your prayer today, ask for refreshment from the presence of the Lord.

> Jesus spoke to the people once more and said, "I am the light of the world. If you follow me, you won't have to walk in darkness, because you will have the light that leads to life."
>
> —John 8:12

2. As you reflect on these verses, ask Holy Spirit to show
    you any place where you have a heaviness, a darkness,
    or some residual pain from situations you have
    experienced. Seek the Lord to find the way He wants to
    lead you out to the life He wants for you.

    > Be anxious for nothing, but in everything by
    > prayer and supplication, with thanksgiving, let
    > your requests be made known to God; and the
    > peace of God, which surpasses all understand-
    > ing, will guard your hearts and minds through
    > Christ Jesus.
    >
    > —Philippians 4:6–7

3. Ask Holy Spirit to help you see where you have become
    a worrier instead of the warrior that He wants you to
    be. Sometimes we simply have to stop begging God
    for Him to move in our lives, make our request from a
    believing heart, and then rest in Him while He works
    it out.

NEW LEGACY

Throughout the medical and physical journey required for John's body to heal, God worked through the people He placed on the path around us. It was amazing to see how much the professional medical staff were touched and moved by the healing miracle that was happening. They were all active, cheering parts of the team that came together to work with John to get him back to full health. The military personnel came to support and encourage us; President Obama and his wife Michelle came to say they cared; and of course, God's family was sent to be around us. God had even relocated our pastor's daughter and son-in-law to walk with us through all of this.

When you are surrounded by an "extended family," it increases your desire to make sure your core family group heals and becomes connected in better ways. There were times before Jesus came into our lives when I couldn't see any way that our kids would all get along and we would have a close, loving family. At one point, Mason and Tia decided not to live with us anymore so they went to live with their biological father. It broke my heart.

God healed the relationship between John and Mason and began to work in our relationships with Tia and John,

Jr. as well. His love and Jesus's words and ways have transformed our family. We couldn't have done what He has done; we tried and were not successful! It touches my heart when I see pictures on Facebook of John, Jr, and Mason together with the caption, "My Brother!" They are not stepbrothers now; they are true brothers. Only God can do that.

Our past doesn't determine our future. Only God does that. He uses the ones the world says are the "wrong kinds of people" to bring about the wonder-filled plan He has. Matthew recorded a most unusual account of the lineage of Jesus in the first chapter of his Gospel account. In the culture of that day, only the men were counted and accounted for in family histories. Matthew, however, lists *women* in Jesus' ancestry. It encourages me when I realize that Tamar acted as a prostitute with her father-in-law, Rehab was a pagan and a prostitute, Ruth also a pagan, married a Jewish man, and Bathsheba's relationship with King David began as an adulterous affair. These grandmothers and great-grandmothers in the Royal Lineage of Jesus, the Savior of the world, were all broken and seemingly unfit for royal positions. I'm sure when they were little girls, they never dreamed of one day being known by the world as part of a Royal Family. But God redeemed and reclaimed their lives and gave them a new legacy. He wants to do that for us all.

God's heart for what He wants for our children and us is shown in Proverbs 17:6, *Grandchildren are the pride and joy of old men and a son is proud of his father.* John and I have been greatly blessed to have sweet grandchildren who share our lives and truly bring us joy. Seeing our children parent their own children brings us great happiness. We know it only happened when we allowed God to come into our souls and heal the darkness. Now that we share His light, our children are being drawn to Him also.

The following quote captured my attention one day. It is a conversation between two caterpillars in a sweet book, *Hope for the Flowers* by Trina Paulus.

> "How does one become a butterfly? Yellow asked pensively.
>
> "You must want to fly so much that you are willing to give up being a caterpillar."
>
> "You mean to die?" asked Yellow.
>
> "Yes and No," he answered. "What **looks** like you will die, but what's **really** you will still live."

This puts into different words the way transformation with the Lord has happened in my life. I had to be willing to stop being who I had always been, so the Lord could change my heart and mind and I could be who He made me to be.

The more I walk with the Lord, reading and studying the Bible, and staying connected to Jesus through prayer and praise, the more I have been changed. The old ways I lived have died out. The old person who was filled with depression and sadness has gone away. I don't identify myself with all the old labels; I don't accept the old limitations. The things of the world don't pull me to them anymore. What I used to be has died, and Jesus has given birth to the person I really am. I'm sure a caterpillar never dreams that one day he will be transformed into a beautiful creature that will gracefully sail through the world. I am at that stage, like a butterfly, where I have crawled out of the darkness, and I am beginning to see my true self and the wonder of who He made me to be; and I am beginning to dream about the wonder of who I am and all the possibilities ahead.

I'm not perfect, and I know I'm not as strong as I will be. But I'm closer than ever before. Just like the butterfly, I will find the courage and God will give me the strength to spread my wings and soar wherever He leads me.

Freedom Exercise:
Read, Reflect, Record

> I have been crucified with Christ; it is no longer I who live, but Christ lives in me; and the life which I now live in the flesh I live by faith in the Son of God, who loved me and gave Himself for me.
>
> —Galatians 2:20

> We know that our old life, our old sinful self, was nailed to the cross with Christ. And so the power of sin that held us was destroyed. Sin is no longer our boss. When a man is dead, he is free from the power of sin.
>
> —Romans 6:6–7

1. Pray these verses over your life. As Holy Spirit leads you, become aware of anything from your old life that you have kept alive. Ask Jesus to forgive you and strengthen your will so you can claim the victory He paid for you to have.

2. As you go about your day, praise Jesus for the work He did on the cross and proclaim the Truth that you are now free!

> Do not remember the things that have happened before. Do not think about the things of the past. See, I will do a new thing. It will begin happening now. Will you not know about it? I will even make a road in the wilderness, and rivers in the desert.
>
> —Isaiah 43:18–19

> Put away the old person you used to be. Have nothing to do with your old sinful life. It was sinful because of being fooled into following bad desires. Let your minds and hearts be made new. You must become a new person and be God-like. Then you will be made right with God and have a true holy life.
>
> —Ephesians 4:22–24

3. Be aware of any regrets, or shame, or embarrassments from your old life. Work with Holy Spirit to once and

for all let them go. Talk to Jesus about any that want to hold you back. Ask what He wants to say to you about them. Visualize all your past being washed by a powerful running stream of clear water until there is no more darkness.

4. Ask Holy Spirit to show you the new life He has for you. Spend time affirming who He says you are. Find verses about His promises, then memorize them so they will stay in your soul and remind you that your new life has been created by Him for you. Ask Him to give you dreams of your new legacy.

†††

PART 5

OPEN THEIR EYES

O Lord, I pray, open his eyes, that he may see."

—2 Kings 6:17

SEEING IS BELIEVING

When Jesus came into our lives, Angel and I began a journey of faith. We decided we would follow Jesus because the path we were traveling was leading to destruction and we had come to believe Jesus offered a better way of living. Those first few years we followed, but we were walking quite a distance away from Him. We had hope in Him because of what we saw in her parents' hearts at their conversion, and we felt more of His presence with us. Some of that time, we were encouraged by the faith walk of the wonderful people God placed in our lives. We had "God glimpses" as our faith grew.

The miraculous healing after the shooting greatly increased our faith. We saw Him do impossible, common sense defying things in my body which left us both wanting to understand Him on a higher level. It wasn't enough anymore to take other people's understanding of Him; we truly wanted to come to know Him. That desire for more directed us to the Bible which led us to find wonderful insights.

Since God audibly told me to "Get Up!" I started to search for His use of that phrase in the Bible. I found several and, interestingly enough, He said that to Paul after He had blinded him on the road to Damascus as recorded in Acts 26:16–18.

> Now **get up** and stand on your feet. I have appeared to you to appoint you as a servant and as a witness of what you have seen and will see of me. I will rescue you from your own people and from the Gentiles. I am sending you to them to **open their eyes** and turn them from darkness to light, and from the power of satan to God, so that they may receive forgiveness of sins and a place among those who are sanctified by faith in me.

Holy Spirit quickened within me. I knew I had a calling on my life. Jesus had spoken to me another time saying, "What are you doing, John?" I was new to spiritually understanding how to listen to Him when He was speaking to me. So, I replied, "What am I doing? Jesus, I don't understand your question. I'm recovering after being shot, I go to my doctor's appointments, and I go to church." God responded, "I didn't save you just so that you could go to church! I saved you to tell the world about me. You are living proof that my ways have not changed. I am still the Creator of miracles. Now go tell my people that I want to do the same for them!" It wasn't long after this encounter with Jesus that I began to do more outside the confines of the church, and He started opening doors that no man could shut.

The verses in Acts were highlighted in my soul. They cemented the purpose of the mission God has given me. Telling of His miracle in my life is the **"how"** of my mission. The **"why"** of my mission is to open people's eyes so they can see God as He is. When they truly see Him, they will turn from the power of satan to embrace a relationship with the Living Christ and be eternally sanctified.

We can't marvel at the wonders of His miracles if we can't see Him. We can't have a relationship with someone we have never seen. If we only walk in darkness, we will never know the beauty the Light reveals to us. With the Light, we can see the unseen.

Freedom Exercise:
Read, Reflect, Record

> Now faith is the substance of things hoped for, the evidence of things not seen. For by it the elders obtained a good testimony. By faith we understand that the worlds were framed by the word of God, so that the things which are seen were not made of things which are visible.
>
> —Hebrews 11:1–3

1. As you sit in His presence today, call to mind all you hope for. Ask Holy Spirit what He wants to say to you about each hope in your heart.

2. Where can you find evidence of the things not seen which you hope for.

> I am sending you to them to open their eyes and turn them from darkness to light, and from the power of satan to God, so that they may receive

forgiveness of sins and a place among those who are sanctified by faith in me.

—Acts 26:18

3. The Christian faith was greatly increased by the work Paul did after His conversion. Clearly, the verse above states the mission God gave him. Talk with the Lord about your life, examining where you are and asking Him to show you how you have turned from darkness to light. Have you fully received forgiveness?

4. Take time to reflect on your faith in Him. How has it made a difference in the way you live your life? How is He using your transformation to touch others?

WHICH EYES?

Jesus, while He was walking on earth, had a great deal to say about people who had eyes but could not see. For instance, when He was talking about the people who were around Him and said, *"For the hearts of these people are hardened, and their ears cannot hear, and they have closed their eyes; so their eyes cannot see, and their ears cannot hear, and their hearts cannot understand."*

It seems hard to understand; you would think that seeing His miracles and hearing His teachings, everyone would have been drawn to them. Yet even His own disciples had a hard time seeing what He meant, and we find the account of that in Mark 8. After He had fed 5,000 with 5 loaves, and 4,000 with 7 loaves, they began to be concerned because they had only brought one loaf of bread on a short trip. Our Savior was a bit taken aback by that. He said, *"Having eyes, do you not see? And having ears, do you not hear? And do you not remember?"* I completely understand how He must have felt. Why are we all like those disciples sometimes? Because sometimes, we keep our Spiritual eyes shut, even though we have seen with our natural eyes the signs and wonders He just performed for us.

Further in Mark 8, there is a description of Jesus healing a blind man. There is some misunderstanding around this account at times.

> Then He came to Bethsaida; and they brought a blind man to Him and begged Him to touch him. So He took the blind man by the hand and led him out of the town. And when He had spit on his eyes and put His hands on him, He asked him if he saw anything. And he looked up and said, "I see men like trees, walking." Then He put His hands on his eyes again and made him look up. And he was restored and saw everyone clearly.

—Mark 8:22–26

This healing of the blind man shows a very critical teaching. There were actually two restorations of sight. The first time was not the man's physical sight that was healed, it was his spiritual sight. He saw men as trees. Many times, throughout Scripture godly men are described as trees. A few of the phrases from verses are: *"He shall be like a tree planted by the rivers of water; I am like an olive tree thriving in the house of God; the godly will flourish like palm trees; these two prophets are the two olive trees;"* and Jesus says of those who follow Him, *"A good tree produces good fruit."*

When this man's spiritual eyes were open, he saw men the way God described them in the ancient texts. Jesus wants to open our Spiritual eyes also. He wants us to see the world the way He does, He wants us to see people the way He sees them so we can love them and minister to them the way He does. He wants us to see Him moving in the unseen on our behalf so that we won't lose hope.

When our spiritual eyes are open, we can see Him as He is and know the things He does in our lives. He has given us all eyes to see. He tells us we are blessed when we see with them, and that prophets and righteous men desired to see what we can see with our spiritual sight.

Freedom Exercise
Read, Reflect, Record

> May the eyes of your understanding being enlightened; that you may know what is the hope of His calling, what are the riches of the glory of His inheritance in the saints, and what is the exceeding greatness of His power toward us who believe, according to the working of His mighty power.
>
> —Ephesians 1:18–19

1. Prayerfully enter into a time of seeking to be closer to the Lord than you were yesterday. Meditate on these verses, letting Him show you the fullness of who He is and the power of His commitment to you.

> The servant of the man of God got up early and went out. And he saw an army with horses and war-wagons around the city. The servant said to Elisha, "It is bad, sir! What should we do?"
> He answered, "Do not be afraid. For those who are with us are more than those who are

> with them." Then Elisha prayed and said, "O Lord, I pray, open his eyes, that he may see." And the Lord opened the servant's eyes, and he saw. He saw that the mountain was full of horses and war-wagons of fire all around Elisha.
>
> —2 Kings 6:15–17

2. Are you walking through a situation having heard, or having said to yourself, "It is bad!" The servant's question of "What should we do?" is answered by Elisha—we should pray! Do that today. Ask the Lord to open your spiritual eyes and let you see where God is in this situation. If you are feeling alone in this, ask to see who else is with you during this time.

3. Whatever you need, ask for it. Perhaps it is wisdom, a friend, understanding, an open door, or the right path. Jesus knows and understands; pour out your heart to him.

4. As you complete your time on this today, be sure to stay aware of watching for what He does in your life; see with your spiritual eyes.

WATCHFUL

Making Jesus the focus of our lives also changed our perspective about what our culture calls "normal." Seeing the goodness and mercy He showed us, truly gave us the desire to live so that our habits and actions would proclaim Him even louder than our words would. Holy Spirit began to change the desires of our hearts; now, we wanted the kingdom life. Neither of us is perfect in living that yet. Following Jesus doesn't mean we will be perfect; in fact, it may mean there will be attacks from the devil more frequently. We may be "attacked at home," but now we will see the enemy for who he is.

The devil is still going to do what the devil does. Often when we come to faith in Christ, satan doesn't want to lose his grip on us. He really doesn't care one way or the other about us. He just wants to take people out of Jesus' kingdom.

The devil is still going to try to entice us. He is still going to try to discount God in our mind so he can rob us of our joy. He is still going to whisper the same vile lies and when we don't listen to him, he will increase his volume until he is roaring lies in our head that become louder than the Truth. Tell him to shut up! No matter what he says to you, you don't have to listen to him. Follow Jesus' example and speak Scripture with all the power of God behind it to silence him.

The first mention of him in Scripture describes him as a serpent who was more cunning than all the wild animals God had created. Angel's comment is that he *must* have been cunning to get a woman to talk to a snake; most women would agree. We must never forget that about him. He can get us to do things we think we would never do. We must see with spiritual eyes because he won't come to us as a grotesque, distorted, evil monster. He will come looking and sounding like something we want.

He uses bright shiny things and creates a perceived "need" for them in our lives when we are struggling to free ourselves from debt. He uses our cultural acceptance that says, "Just one beer won't hurt," to try to drag someone back into addiction. He will use an attractive co-worker who "understands you" to kill off a marriage that God formed. Often he will use success after success in the worldly realm to show us we don't need God; we are very capable. He will even use religion to foster a self-righteous attitude to destroy our relationship with Jesus. He is cunning and will use whatever grabs you in your weakest area to be able to devour you and God's plan and purpose for your life. We need to open our spiritual eyes and see the vile, grotesque hand offering us the way to our destruction.

Freedom Exercise:
Read, Reflect, Record

Be of sober spirit, be on the alert. Your adversary, the devil, prowls around like a roaring lion, seeking someone to devour.

—1 Peter 5:8

Keep watch and pray, so that you will not give in to temptation. For the spirit is willing, but the body is weak!

—Matthew 26:41

So humble yourselves before God. Resist the devil, and he will flee from you.

—James 4:7

1. Prayerfully read through these verses. Ask Holy Spirit to increase your concern about the devil, asking to see any place where you have let your guard down. Have you shut your spiritual eyes?

2. As you meditate on these verses, allow them to show you areas where you are being tempted or are being weak. Is there any place where you haven't become humble before God? Ask for Holy Spirit strengthening.

> You were formerly darkness, but now you are Light in the Lord; walk as children of Light.
>
> —Ephesians 5:8

3. This verse reminds us that we are all His children. The easiest animal for a roaring lion to pick off is the one separated from the herd. If you are being dragged back into the dark, ask Jesus to show you where you are not connected to other children of Light.

4. Ask to see strongholds you have in your soul which have not been broken. Define what attitudes, lies, labels, and limitations you are holding onto. We cannot defeat whatever we don't define. Ask for Scripture to tear those strongholds down.

5. Meditate on this verse, asking to see what your life would be like if you fully became Light in the world around you.

FAITH BRINGS SIGHT

Scripture tells us that we overcome by the blood of the Lamb and the word of our testimony. Angel and I have many testimonies which prove God's power to transform lives. Psalm 103 reminds us of the benefits of being His children.

> Let all that I am praise the Lord; may I never forget all His benefits. He forgives all my sins and heals all my diseases. He redeems me from death and crowns me with love and tender mercies. He fills my life with good things. My youth is renewed like the eagle's.

We can stand and boldly testify that we have seen, with natural and spiritual eyes, that he has shown every one of those benefits in our marriage, in our family, in our finances, and in our careers. Now, he is honoring us by allowing us to walk into a world that is hurting, speak into the lives of people, and hear their testimonies as He touches their souls when they Get Up to follow him.

We are including two testimonies from special people we have encountered in our journey, but there are so many more. We want to encourage you to share your testimonies. It is how Jesus is built up, not only in the lost world, but also in the hearts of our brothers and sisters in Christ. If He is high and lifted up, *He* will draw all men to Himself. One of our tasks, while we are on this Spiritual Special Forces mission, is to lift Him up by sharing the good news of what He did on the cross and in our lives because of it. We must lift Him up as often and as high as we can.

Arrested by His Love

I would never have thought that Jesus could use my life's trials to bring healing and comfort to others. He had His hands full with my family and me. Yet now He uses our testimonies to encourage, set free, call to action, and deliver those He is restoring.

An outdoors ministry invited me to be the keynote speaker during a weekend retreat for First Responders from Los Angeles and Texas. First Responders really need encouragement these days, which is why I accepted the invitation. This ministry reaches people through and during outdoor activities. Typically, during hunting or fishing excursions, the guide will use the time together to establish a relationship with the participant, listen to them, and share the love of Christ. They have had a front-row seat to God's faithfulness, restoration, and healing.

At this particular event, we were not sure how to engage the police officers. We were unsure of their beliefs. There were a lot of unknowns. First of all, they usually do not trust people. It is their job to be suspicious. I invited a close friend and mentor, who was also a minister and former Texas State Trooper, to join me on the trip. I was sure they would feel comfortable around him.

When we arrived at the lodge we were met by the director. He said, "Let's take a ride and talk." He showed us their beautiful property and we discussed our approach. We agreed we wouldn't go in on "Full Auto" with the Gospel, but we would establish a relationship and let the guys relax. We finished our tour and arrived back at the lodge. I went in and grabbed a snack and sat down. Within minutes, the officer from Texas sat next to me. He made small talk then said, "I know your story." I was surprised, but it was a perfect opening, so I said, "Since you know my story tell me yours."

He said, "I was shot several years ago while trying to make entry into a building." He continued by sharing his story of how he had nearly died after being shot. The trauma had affected him emotionally and it was hard for him to connect with counselors because he did not feel they could relate to his situation and trauma. I cannot recall how the conversation changed directions, but I began to talk about forgiveness. I explained that I was able to move forward in my healing only after Jesus helped me forgive the soldier that shot me. Unforgiveness can create a root of bitterness in you and that root can manifest itself in depression, addictions, fear, anxiety, and anger. He had also experienced several of those emotions.

I asked, "Are you willing to forgive the man that shot you?" I thought he would say, "No way!" I was wrong; he quickly responded, "Yes!" We began to pray, and he forgave the man that shot him. When he lifted his head after the prayer and looked at me, he had a huge smile on his face. He was completely set free! The next morning, he told me, "Last night was the first peaceful sleep I have had in a long time. I called my wife and told her I am a new man."

Here's how I saw the miraculous happen. I thought we needed a plan to engage the police officers. The truth is, God wanted to "arrest" those men with His love. He needed me to put my agenda aside and let Him work through me. He did the work.

Send Me to Those Who Have Been Forgotten

We were contacted by a pastor who was hoping to coordinate a large outreach. He wanted to reach the veterans, bikers, and the *"whosoevers"* in his community. To ensure my husband John was the right speaker for his event, the pastor drove five hours to Fort Worth, TX to meet with us. Most people coordinate with us through phone calls and emails. But this pastor needed to be sure we were legit, anointing and all. After our meeting and praying together he was satisfied. It was set. "Let's win the lost for Christ!" he said.

When the time had come, we drove five hours to the church. We arrived in time to check into our hotel and rest a bit. John was scheduled to speak at 3:00 pm and again at 6:00 pm. He called the pastor to let him know we had arrived. Then I heard John say, "Okay pastor, well, keep me posted. We will be waiting for your call." I felt something was not right, but I did not want to share my concern. John ended the call then looked at me and said, "No one showed up for the rally except for the church staff and members." My mouth dropped! "What are we going to do?" I asked. He said, "Whatever the pastor wants. We did not drive five hours for nothing." Our morale and our attitude dropped during the time spent waiting. Three o" clock came and went with no word from the pastor. Finally, at 5:45 pm, John's phone rang, and he heard the discouraged pastor say in a low tone, "Come on over."

The drive over to the church was not filled with enthusiasm. As we drove, John began to complain and then said, "I need to pray more about the invites I accept." As we pulled up to the building, we were immediately met by the pastor. He started apologizing and seemed a bit embarrassed. John said, "Pastor, do not worry about anything we are here now. Let's make the best of it."

The church was beautiful inside even though the community around it appeared to be in a low-income area. Church members were warm and welcoming as they came to greet us. We were getting settled and John had just told the pastor that we had our books for sale. Then suddenly, I heard John saying, "Pastor, you guys will not buy our books. They are FREE!" I thought to myself, "We just drove five hours, and you are going to give our books away?"

John walked up to me with tears in his eyes. I asked, "What happened?" He said, "I felt the Lord say, 'You asked Me for this.' When the church members started greeting us the Lord reminded me of what I prayed recently, "*Lord, send me to those who have been forgotten.*" John was overwhelmed with emotions because he knew that we were there because of his prayer. The world looked down on this church and its members which is why no one attended their event. But God! He knows who they are. It humbled us that He sent us five hours from Fort Worth, Texas, to share His love with them. Our attitudes completely changed. Needless to say, we repented and quickly asked for forgiveness.

John spoke, and there was an overwhelming response from people. At the end, John began praying for anyone who came forward. There was a young couple who held back, waiting for everyone to finish. Finally, the man approached John asking, "Will you pray for me?" John said, "Of course, but what about her?" nodding toward the young woman. "She does not want prayer," the guy answered. John prayed for him and then finished with everyone else. However, as we were preparing to leave, the same young man returned. "My girlfriend would like to talk with you," he told John. I kept talking to other people when I saw John walk over to speak with the young girl. I kept them in my line of sight in case John might need me. Within a few minutes, John came over and asked me, "Can you speak with the young girl? She is struggling emotionally because she recently lost her father, and she does not know how to handle it." I was taken back because that's exactly what I went through. "Yes, of course, I would love to speak with her," I said. I spent some time with the young girl sharing and encouraging her. After our talk, we hugged, and I could tell she was calmer and more at peace. John and I packed up, said our good-byes, and left with a sense we had accomplished what God had sent us to do.

We realized God had us drive five hours to a church not many took notice of—but He did. He sent us on a journey for one young girl who was struggling emotionally from nearly the exact situation that had been a struggle for me. His Word is proved out in our lives time after time. This verse from 2 Corinthians 1:4 captures God's purpose. *He comforts us in all our troubles so that we can comfort others. When they are troubled, we will be able to give them the same comfort God has given us.* We realized that there are no limits to the distance God will go to reach and restore and comfort His people.

Freedom Exercise:
Read, Reflect, Record

> "Blessed be the God and Father of our Lord Jesus Christ, the Father of mercies and God of all comfort, who comforts us in all our affliction so that we will be able to comfort those who are in any affliction with the comfort with which we ourselves are comforted by God."
>
> —2 Corinthians 1:3–4

1. Prayerfully recall those times in your life when God comforted you, praising Him for showing you that great mercy. Let Holy Spirit prompt you to be aware of other people you may encounter who need to be comforted by you.

> For this reason, I kneel before the Father, from whom every family in heaven and on earth derives its name. I pray that out of his glorious riches he may strengthen you with power through his Spirit in your inner being, so that Christ may dwell in your hearts through faith.

> And I pray that you, being rooted and established in love, may have power, together with all the Lord's holy people, to grasp how wide and long and high and deep is the love of Christ, and to know this love that surpasses knowledge that you may be filled to the measure of all the fullness of God.
>
> —Ephesians 3:14–19

2. Meditate on these verses, letting them wash you with a deep awareness of Christ living in your heart. Ask the Lord to show you the magnitude of His love for you. Let it fill you with His fullness.

3. Take time to flip back through the pages of this book and your journal letting it remind you of this journey with Him. Take time to store your new awareness deep into your mind and your emotions. End this time with Him in praise of Him for His great love for you.

CONCLUSION

Get up! Get up! I heard those words twice as I fought for each breath, not knowing which would be my last. I have thought back to that very moment. Why did I hear get up twice? The best explanation I have for that is that I did not listen the first time. When those bullets were flying and chaos and death were present, many questioned, "God, where are you?" I now understand and can answer that question. He was in the middle of it all *speaking to me,* encouraging me to fight while I was on the ground and my life was pouring out.

This book was written for your eyes to be opened to the miraculous power of God. Have you heard, Get up? Has someone crossed your path that pointed out that Jesus was there in your situation? Do you know He still has not left you? If not, Angel and I want you to know, you were never alone. Now it's time to Get Up. Please, do not follow my example and wait to be told a second time. Let these words produce action in your physical body, emotional well-being, and your spirit.

If your spiritual eyes have been opened, you have seen the living God. When you see Him as He is, you see what He has been doing to get you to come into a relationship with Him. It is impossible to miss His majesty and His power to work miracles all around you. If you came out of darkness, you may have had your hope devoured by the enemy of your soul. But when those spiritual eyes open up, they show His children the plan He has made and *that* restores their hope!

> May the Lord bless you and keep you. May the Lord make his face to shine upon you and be gracious to you. May the Lord lift up his countenance upon you and give you peace.

Shalom

ABOUT THE AUTHORS
JOHN AND ANGEL ARROYO

Captain John M. Arroyo U. S. Army (Ret.) and his wife **Angel** live in Burleson, Texas. John graduated with a B. S. from Campbell University in North Carolina and an M. A. from SUM Bible college and theological seminary in Sacramento, California. Angel graduated with a B. A. in theology from Texas University of Theology in Hurst, Texas. John travels extensively, speaking at churches, military installations, civic centers, and schools. His message about resiliency in the face of overwhelming odds has resonated with all of his audiences, and he is a much sought-after speaker.

ABOUT THE CO-AUTHOR
PEGGY CORVIN

 Freedom minister, speaker, teacher, and family life trainer, Peggy passionately brings freedom to Christian believers through applied Scripture and the power of God's Light. Her Master's degree in theology from Kings University and a B.A. in education and early childhood specialties have equipped her to know how to break strongholds that form in the spiritual lives of Christians. She particularly loves helping other women find their silenced voices and tell of their journeys out of darkness into God's light. Peggy lives near Nashville, Tennessee, with her husband Stan, their kids, and grandchildren.